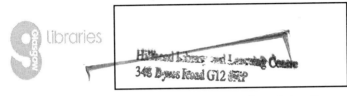
This book is due for return on or before the last date shown below. It may be renewed by telephone, personal application, fax or post, quoting this date, author, title and the book number

Glasgow Life and its service brands, including Glasgow Libraries, (found at www.glasgowlife.org.uk) are operating names for Culture and Sport Glasgow

Glasgow
CITY COUNCIL

THE
FIVE-
A-SIDE
BIBLE

Inside the world of tasty tackles
and terrible touches

THE FIVE-A-SIDE BIBLE

Inside the world of tasty tackles
and terrible touches

FREIGHT
BOOKS

BACKPAGE

First published in 2015 by BackPage and Freight Books

Freight Books
49-53 Virginia Street
Glasgow, G1 1TS
www.freightbooks.co.uk

BackPage
www.backpagepress.co.uk
@BackPagePress

Copyright © Chris Bruce, 2015
Illustrations by Dave Alexander
Photography by Bob McDevitt

ISBN: 978-1-910449-28-8

the publisher acknowledges investment from
Creative Scotland toward the publication of this book

Printed and bound by Hussar Books

To my family, Alle and Cameron
– the best team I could have picked

Contents

The Best Team Names Ever

What's your first priority when starting a 5-a-side team? Kit? Tactics? Forget it. It's all about picking the right team name. Witty, rude, downright offensive – combine all three and you've really cracked it

Murder On Zidane's Floor	The Neville wears Prada
Maradonna Kebab	Agger Diouf Diouf Diouf
Petr Cech Yourself	Le Saux Solid Crew
Chamakh My Pitch Up	Baines on Toast
Mirror Signal Malouda	Michu at De Gea Ba
Xavi Dodgers	Hakuna Juan Mata
Haven't Got a Kalou	Sex and Drugs and Carlton Cole
Jimmyfloydbottlebaink	Debbie does Gallas

Balotellitubbies

Slumdog Mignolet

This is Sparta Prague

50 Shades of O'Shea

Alice in Hangeland

One Size Fitz Hall

Tea and Busquets

Sevilla Lacatalent

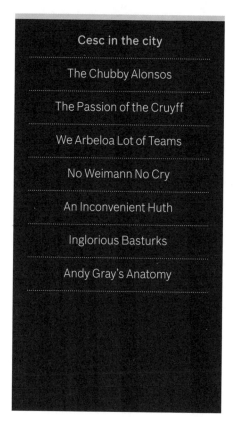

Cesc in the city

The Chubby Alonsos

The Passion of the Cruyff

We Arbeloa Lot of Teams

No Weimann No Cry

An Inconvenient Huth

Inglorious Basturks

Andy Gray's Anatomy

Go ahead, *you* tell him you didn't do your homework.

Kindergarten
COP

Kindergarten Klopp	Ozil Gummidge
Bolton Fondlers	Romasexuals
Crystal Phallus	Rodallega Bombs
Old 'n' Pathetic / Oldman Arthritic	Pathetico Madrid
Stroke Titty	Beercelona
Breast Homage Albion	Osasuna Or Later
AC A Little Silhouette Of Milan	Real Sosobad / Real Sociopaths
Enter 'Me Lamb / Inter Your Nan	ACDC United

Athletic Bilbao Baggins	Colonel Getafe
Sporting Abeergut / Sporting Lesbian	Werder Beermen
Bayern Bru Bayer Neverlosen	Expected Toulouse
Borussia Mönchenflapjack / Monster Munchen Gladbach	Paris Ganja Man
Bayern Eunuch	Paralympique Marseille
Benteke Fried Chicken	Ivory Toast
Hangover 96	Tekkerslovakia
	Shitzerland

Kings of Lyon	Cameroon Diaz
Basement Ajax	Red Balls Salzburg
Parmesan Belgrade	Rapid Viennetta
Boca Seniors	Lesbian Lions
Mentalist Kharkiv	Law Abiding Sigurddsons
Substandard Liege	Phallus Cowboys
Olympiadross	Tittsburgh Feelers
Cry me a River Plate	Club Tropicana Drinks FC

Fiorentina Turner	Teenage Mutant Ninja Skrtels
Multiple Scoregasms	Champagne Super Rovers
99 Problems But a Pitch Ain't One	Scouting For Goals
Sons of Pitches	Phantom of the Chopra
Obi 1 Kenobi nil	Kiss My Pass
Ball of Duty	The Fashion Pulis
ABCDE F.C	2 goals 1 cup
It's Spraining Men	Egoala

Le God says...

Let there be 5-a-side!

We caught up with Matt Le Tissier to find out how one of the Premier League's great entertainers keeps his hand in at his local Goals – and how fives gave him an early taste of the big time

The memory of Matt Le Tissier hipswaying past defenders is still enough to make purists quiver. To Southampton fans, he remains 'Le God', a football deity who illuminated the English top-flight in a stellar career from the late 1980s to the early noughties.

Is it any wonder, then, that the first midfielder to score 100 goals in the Premier League still pulls on his boots every week for a kickabout with his mates? Le Tissier, now in his mid-40s, plays in a regular 5-a-side game with friends, former team-mates and family members. It is little surprise to hear that his quick feet and eye for a goal are well suited to the smaller-sided game...

**You still play 5-a-side.
Where is your game?**
We play at Goals in Southampton, which is a very good set-up. I started in 2013 when I had lost a bit of weight and needed to get my fitness up. We play every Tuesday and usually get 12 bodies. We play 5-a-side with one sub, which gives everyone a little rest. My son plays in goal for our team and I fill the rest of the team up with a couple of mates and a couple of ex-players. We've got a lot of players of different standards. From

myself, who's played at international level, to a couple who played at Premier League level, others who played in the lower leagues and then guys who played parks football. The ex-pros are normally in my team. We're all in our mid-40s but we can compensate for our lack of pace with our experience. The nucleus of the teams is the same every week and the games are always pretty tight. We never have a ref. We always just ref ourselves and, in the last year, there's been less than 10 free-kicks given. So, football is better when there's no refs!

My son plays in goal and I fill the team with mates and ex-pros

Matt Le Tissier in his pomp at Southampton
© Getty images

5-a-side participation levels are now higher than 11-a-side. Can you understand the appeal?

I completely understand. It is more convenient. You can do it in the evening after work and don't need to give up a day of your weekend. 11s can also be a struggle if you're not as fit, but you can get away with it in fives. One of my mates I play golf with refuses to play in the winter. So, October to March, I would never see him, but he comes along and plays in goals at the 5-a-side. We usually stick around after the game and have a drink, and if there's a live football game on, we will watch that. It's a nice social thing to do.

What position do you play?

I move about a bit. For half the game I'll be playing as the striker and then for the other half I might play at the back, pass it about a bit and have a breather! Because the parks are so small, you can change places very quickly.

Most professionals look forward to the 5-a-side game at the end of training more than anything. There was always a real edge to the games and it could get tasty. I've always enjoyed small-sided games. You need good control and be able to wriggle out of small spaces, so maybe it is suited to me.

What 11-a-side skills translate well to 5-a-side?

When it comes to finishing, the skills needed for 5-a-side and 11s are similar. You have to know where the goal is and know where the goalkeeper is.

There are other moments in games which mirror 11s. It's about keeping control of the ball when there are lots of people around you. In that sense, it's like playing a whole 11-a-side game in the penalty box!

A good goalkeeper is key, particularly someone who doesn't mind having the ball shot at them from five yards out.

It's also good if you have a couple of guys who know where the goal is, and another couple who can defend quite well and keep the ball – possession is a big thing in 5-a-side.

Did you play 5-a-side when you were growing up?

I played at the leisure centre in Guernsey and also for the Methodist youth club. Our Methodist club actually entered the national 5-a-side tournament and got all the way through to the final at the Royal Albert Hall – I have actually played 5-a-side in the Royal Albert Hall! I think we won the nationals twice actually. We had a strong team, two of my older brothers played in it too.

What advice would you give to help 5-a-side players improve?

My advice is not to be frightened to take a chance. You are not always certain to score a goal, but you need to take chances. If that means shooting through legs then that's what you have to do. Don't be too careful in front of goal. Even if you miss, you'll always get another chance soon.

I have played 5-a-side in the Royal Albert Hall – I think we won the nationals twice

Matt Le Tissier's

Southampton Dream Team

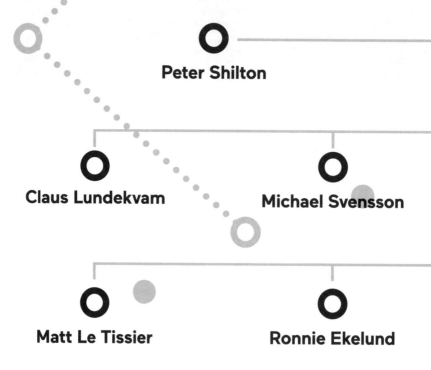

Peter Shilton

Claus Lundekvam

Michael Svensson

Matt Le Tissier

Ronnie Ekelund

Shilton
Record England caps, and
I played alongside him for
a couple of seasons

Lundekvam and Svensson
The centre-back partnership
when we got to the FA Cup
final in 2003. Rock solid

Ekelund
He was right on my wavelength,
we got on like a house on fire

Le Tissier
I'd have to pick myself

Pirlo v Hazard

5-a-side
Dream Team

Our Verdict – Pirlo win

Hazard's cavalier tactics cost him dearly as the Maldini-Nesta axis soaks up the pressure and Ronaldo scores a hat-trick

Gianluigi Buffon

Paolo Maldini

Alessandro Nesta

Andrea Pirlo

Ronaldo
(the Brazilian one)

Source: UEFA.com

Source: Chelseafc.com

Demba Ba

Didier Drogba

Juan Mata

Gervinho

Thibaut Courtois

The Master of 5-a-side

John Durnin was a fringe player at Liverpool in the 1980s. He could never oust Aldridge, Barnes and Rush but when it came to the small-sided game he surpassed them all

In 2000, Sky Sports started showing Masters Cup football – an indoor small-sided tournament for older and ex-pros. It became essential viewing for fans eager to glimpse club legends at varying levels of fitness. Some icons burnished their status by proving that their 11-a-side skills could translate into the small-sided game. Others who were never headline acts in the big leagues, became legends in their own right.

John Durnin began his career at Liverpool – breaking Ian Rush's reserve goalscoring record and getting a few first-team run-outs – but failed to force his way into a side which was then the dominant force in English football. However, as part of the excellent Liverpool Masters team – featuring John Barnes, John Aldridge, Ronnie Whelan and Rush – Durnin bookended his career as a journeyman striker with Oxford, Portsmouth and Port Vale with an impressive reign of dominance in the Masters Cup.

The former Liverpool apprentice picked up the Masters Golden Boot – awarded to the tournament's top goalscorer – twice. His Liverpool team also won the Masters Cup twice during the noughties. It may have taken longer than he expected, but Durnin had finally claimed a little place in Liverpool's history.

John, tell us about how you came to play for the Liverpool Masters side?
Someone dropped out of the Liverpool team for the tournament in London and the Masters phoned me by chance. I was 36 or 37 the first time I played and one of the fittest. I took the place by storm. I scored 11 or 12 goals in the tournament. Then the Masters just grew and grew. In the first 10 years, Liverpool won it twice and got to the final a few times.

01

01 Durnin being presented
with the Golden Boot

02 The victorious 2002
Liverpool Masters Team.
Back row (l-r) Aldridge,
Rush, Molby, Spackman,
Walsh, Bolder. Bottom
row (l-r) Neal, Durnin,
Kennedy, Case

03 Liverpool celebrate
winning the 2002
Masters Cup

Mickey Thomas was outstanding. Mike Marsh played, too, and we had a telepathic understanding.

Every year we travelled abroad to the Far East and Canada. We would go away for a week, stay in a nice hotel and have all our expenses paid. It was a great life experience.

Liverpool were one of the most dominant teams in the Masters and you were their star striker. What was the secret to the team's – and your personal – success?

At Liverpool in the 80s, all we did at training was play 5-a-side. We used to all warm up as a group – the first team, reserves and youths. We would do a couple of laps of Melwood at a steady pace and then all stretch in a circle. Then do two more laps. Then have a game of 5-a-side. We would stop for a bit and do 50-yard sprints – then back to 5-a-side. It sounds easy but it wasn't.

Playing 5-a-side at Liverpool was all about two touches, passing and moving. You had to be on the move all the time. If you stood still you got screamed at. If you took three or four touches, the coaches slaughtered you. Your brain was working all the time, your touch had to be spot on. If you watched the Liverpool first team in the 80s, everyone was passing and moving.

The hardest thing in 5-a-side is chasing the ball. If you don't have the ball you get tired quickly. If you look at the old Masters tapes, you'll see that we rarely gave the ball away. We just probed and probed and probed, and knew when to make the forward pass.

I am staring at the Masters Golden Boot right now! The first name on it was Ally McCoist (2000), John Taylor won it for Bradford in 2001, Peter Beardsley the next year and then I won it from 2004 to 2006. A lot of finishing is instinct.

The small-sided game – whether it be five- six- or seven-a-side – is radically different from 11-a-side. How would you try and improve an average 5-a-side team?

You've got to have a 'cat' in goals. That can make a big difference in a tight games where the first goal is important. Very often if the keeper makes a great save then the other team will go up the other end and score, and usually go on to win 2- or 3-0.

At Liverpool in the 80s all we did at training was play 5-a-side

There was a local 5-a-side team near me in Warrington who were going in for a tournament with some money at stake. I agreed I would coach them up to the tournament, and I took them for three nights a week over two weeks. I watched them closely and they were all trying to run with the ball, so I made it pass-pass-pass. They won the tournament easily. I said to them that you can only run with the ball in 11s, and even then it can be difficult. They used to say at Liverpool: 'What is faster – a pass, or you running with the ball?' The amount of time players get injured from running with the ball and then crazy tackles coming in…

You enjoyed a successful career away from Liverpool. How do you reflect on your career?
I signed for Liverpool when I was 19, in 1985-86. Liverpool won the Double in 1986. I was on the fringes of the first team that season, on the bench, and came on a few times. I played really well in the reserves and broke Ian Rush's goalscoring record. In 88 reserve appearances I scored 69 goals. I was there for four years but they had Rush, Beardsley, Barnes, Aldridge. There was no squad rotation in those days – like there is now – and people played with injuries so that they wouldn't lose their place.

By the third year I was getting frustrated and moved to Oxford. It was brilliant. Everyone hated coming to the Manor Ground and we should have done better with the team we had. Jim Magilton and Mark Stein played in that era. We fought relegation the first year and then were always in the top 10 after that. Then I had eight years at Portsmouth under Jim Smith.

My last club was Port Vale. I went for a coaching job there when I was 37 and Brian Horton was manager. They had a small squad so he asked me to sign a playing contract and I ended up playing 60-odd games until I was 39! My last couple of years were in midfield.

Do you still play?
I play every other week with Jan Molby's local 5-a-side team. The game is in the Wirral. Mickey Thomas plays in it, too. Everyone wants to beat us. We've won it twice in the last four years and finished runners-up in the other two.

And are you still involved in football?
I coached at the Bolton academy for four years and I now coach in Scandinavia in the summer as part of Liverpool's soccer schools. It's all about the ball and how you control it, the technique of how to pass, the weight of it. I don't know what clubs do today, but it is the only way for me. If you want to improve your touch, there is nothing better than 5-a-side.

mastersfootball.com

The 5-a-side Bucket List

We went looking for the most exotic and unusual 5-a-side pitches on the planet. Here's the top four. Put your boots in your backpack and hit the road. Tick them off when you're done

■ ■ ■ ■

Thailand   Cape Town   China   Japan

Showboating
Thailand

Want to cut out overhit passes and wayward shots from your game? Having a kickabout on this floating football pitch in Koh Panyee in Thailand's southern Phang Nga province should focus the mind.

Bring your snorkel

© Christophe Archambault (Getty)

Peak Performance

South Africa

There can be fewer more spectacular backdrops for a game of 5-a-side than Table Mountain in Cape Town, South Africa's most iconic landmark. Stay focused, though. You're on the fives pitch, not the tourist trail

© Taz Raza

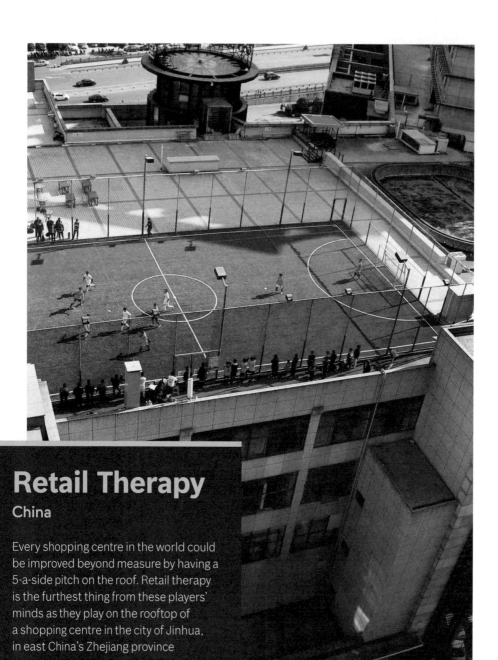

Retail Therapy
China

Every shopping centre in the world could be improved beyond measure by having a 5-a-side pitch on the roof. Retail therapy is the furthest thing from these players' minds as they play on the rooftop of a shopping centre in the city of Jinhua, in east China's Zhejiang province

© Ge yuejin (Imaginechina)

Tokyo Nights
Japan

The Adidas Futsal Park is perched on top of the Tokyu department store, beside Shibuya Station in Tokyo. The facility opened in 2001 ahead of the World Cup in Japan and South Korea in 2002 and remains popular. If you sky a shot, however, it may cause a pile-up at one of the city's busiest intersections below

Tales from the pitch

The Good Samaritan

by Jack Clarence

As 'The Organiser' of our weekly 5-a-side game, everyone looks to me when someone hasn't turned up. If it goes to five past the hour, I text the missing player. "On your way?" If it ticks towards 10 past the hour, I phone them. One night my pal, Wrighty, hadn't turned up.

"Where is he?" asked a few of the boys. Instinctively, you know the guys who have probably forgotten all about it and buggered off to the cinema or some such. Then there are 'the reliables' who you know are probably fighting through traffic jams and flash floods to make it. Wrighty is in the latter group. Sure enough, nine minutes past the hour, Wrighty's car screeches up.

"Sorry, lads, someone was stabbed outside my front door," he says. At the end, he tells us the full tale. He comes out of his flat to find a man slumped against the door of his tenement. "I think I've been stabbed," says the guy. Wrighty calls an ambulance.

Then he spies blood spurting from the guy's back. Wrighty grabs a towel to stem the flow. Good Samaritan. But a Good Samaritan with a 5-a-side game to get to. At this point, a relative of the assailant arrives and starts screaming at the victim that if he has any thoughts about calling the police, he will end up in an even worse condition.

Wrighty looks at his watch. Others have started to gather, he can hear the ambulance sirens and his car is in the middle of a crime scene. Time to cut his losses and get to 5-a-side. We still hold Wrighty up as an example to all latecomers – he is the guy who saved a man's life and still managed to avoid the dreaded 10-past phonecall.

The Road to Rio
(and back again)

Think Brazil 2014 was another World Cup failure for England? Think again. One 5-a-side team from London won two trips to Rio during an all-conquering season. Their goalkeeper lets us in on their secrets

During 2014, the most successful 5–a–side team in the UK was a group of guys by the name of West 13. They had a phenomenal year, winning just about every major tournament there was.

01

Telling us about the amazing run they went on and the incredible prizes they won – including not one, but two trips to Brazil for the World Cup – is their goalkeeper, Ashoor. He's played 5-a-side competitively for around seven years and has seen it all with West 13.

It seems like you've been winning nearly everything in UK 5-a-side for the last couple of years. What's the secret?
It's been unbelievable. First and foremost you've got to have the ability; if you don't then you're going to struggle. But the difference is we've got balance to our team and we work together. There's no envying or hating of each other; we're a team and we want everyone to do well. That really puts us in a good position where we're playing for one another.

Attacking, defending, even off the pitch, we're all supporting each other.

I can't remember a time when two of our players have had a full-blown argument. It has always been constructive and whenever there have been any obstacles in our way we've managed to overcome them by communicating with each other.

We've also got experience. We know how to win the big tournaments and there's confidence within the team. We know what we need to do, and if we're patient and confident in our ability we know we can come out on top.

We played in a tournament to win a trip to Brazil and faced a very good side in the knockout games. We found ourselves a goal down with a minute or two to go. A lot of teams will try and force it in those situations and lose their heads, but we kept plugging away and got an equaliser in the last seconds. Then we beat them on penalties and ended up winning a trip to Brazil!

The other thing is that we've got no weaknesses. Some teams might have a defender who is not strong or a striker who is not prolific, but we've got a balanced squad which is what you need for 5-a-side.

Tell us of some of the stuff you've won playing 5-a-side

Where do I start? In 2014 we won a tournament that took us to Dubai, then we won two trips to Brazil and after that we won a trip to Barcelona. On top of all of that we won a couple of £1000 cash tournaments.

You're just regular guys but you're disappearing on all these exotic holidays just from playing 5-a-side. How does that feel?

It's just a lovely story. My work have been very supportive about it and know that these things are once-in-a-lifetime opportunities. The chance to watch the World Cup in Brazil doesn't come along every day.

Some of the boys have had nightmares with wives and girlfriends though. Telling them they're off on all these lads' holidays to places like Dubai and Brazil isn't easy. It's not exactly like you've been called out to Afghanistan or Iraq is it?

They might be once-in-a-lifetime opportunities, but you went to Brazil twice in 2014!

Yes, there were two different tournaments and both had the prize of going to watch the World Cup in Brazil. The trips were both on different dates, with about 10 days in between them. Some of our lads came home between the two and I don't even think they bothered unpacking.

It would've made sense for us to stay out there and save the two tournament sponsors flying us both there and back but that wasn't an option.

It was the trip of a lifetime, but some of us had done so much travelling that we didn't even want to go on the second trip. That sounds crazy, but we were just wanting to let someone else have a go. We've been very fortunate to have so many opportunities.

02

03

The Architect of 5-a-side

Keith Rogers

In 1987, young Scottish entrepreneur Keith Rogers transformed an underused tennis court into a 5-a-side pitch with his own hands. What happened next changed the way you play the game

If you play 5-a-side football, you may very well play it in a purpose-built facility, like Goals or Powerleague. Those two brands dominate the 3G-landscape of 5-a-side in the UK, and they share the same origin story – it's quite a tale.

Without this story, the explosion of 5-a-side might have happened – but perhaps not. Maybe there'd be far fewer of us playing. Maybe we'd be hiring out school halls and leisure centres and chasing a fuzzy, fluorescent ball around on an unforgiving wooden floor.

Keith Rogers was running a health and fitness club in the Glasgow area when he converted four tennis courts for 5-a-side use. This was the gold-rush moment, the discovery of an untapped market of recreational footballers by a business brain who would spend the next 25 years as the primary influencer in the expansion of 5-a-side into the vibrant football culture it is today.

That health and fitness club became the first centre in the Pitz chain. Pitz became Powerleague after Rogers sold his business to a venture capital firm, and he started over again with Goals.

01

The path of both of the big players started out on the same under-used tennis court in Paisley.

Today he spends his time between the UK and USA, where he is laying the foundation for a new 5-a-side explosion to keep pace with the biggest soccer boom in North American history. This is how it all happened.

How did you come up with the idea of constructing the first purpose-built 5-a-side facility in the UK?

Before the late 80s, if you wanted to play football you booked an indoor hall, were squeezed in between the badminton players and bribed the receptionist for a bit of time. It was a wooden floor with 50 different coloured lines and parallel bars on the wall. I was involved in a health and fitness club which had four tennis courts, but neither myself nor my mates played tennis. So we converted four tennis courts into four 5-a-side courts.

We didn't design it in a particular way. It was more a case of, 'Let's put some timber boards around the tennis courts … hang on, it gets dark around 6pm and people want to play … OK, let's dig a hole and put some lights in'.

Then we said, 'The ball keeps going out of play – let's put a fence around the pitch'. So we solved the problems as we went along until suddenly, after a year, we looked out and said, 'Wow, that's a 5-a-side pitch'. The 5-a-side pitch invented itself.

Once we had the first pitches completed with zero problems we moved to six pitches then 10, all the while being surprised by how popular the game was and how quickly the pitches filled. We realised we were making more money from 5-a-side football than we were from the health and fitness club. So we closed the club and turned it into a football centre.

Having established a successful centre in Paisley, did you then realise the huge potential?

We approached several banks, explained our idea and pointed out that we had a centre in Paisley which we had built ourselves. Several banks passed on giving us a loan because they couldn't imagine a 5-a-side centre as a viable business idea.

In the end, we contacted Scottish & Newcastle Brewers who loved the idea and, on a dark week night in winter, a contingent came up to Glasgow on a bus. It was one of those nights where the rain was blowing sideways in a gale. Every single 5-a-side pitch was full. There were people waiting to get on, people coming off. You could see the penny drop with the Scottish & Newcastle contingent and it was obvious that they were in.

They took me for lunch to a restaurant in Edinburgh called Fat Sam's which had newly opened. As we sat in the restaurant I said, 'Let me tell you the future. This restaurant won't be here in five years but I can guarantee you that the 5-a-side football centre will still be there in 20 years'. I was proven right. The facility in Paisley has been standing for 30 years and is still hosting 5-a-side football every night of the week. Scottish & Newcastle Brewers came on board as a shareholder and they made the introduction to the bank, so suddenly things began to move quicker.

02

From there, we opened a centre in Glasgow and one in Edinburgh, on the site of the old Portobello swimming pool **(above)** which was close to the beach. In those early days the players would get annoyed when the sand from the beach blew onto the pitch. I remember our advertising campaign on local radio around the time of the 1990 World Cup.

We used the *Nessun Dorma* World Cup anthem with the words "our socks are blue our strips are yellow, we play 5-a-side down at Portobello". It was so cheesy that it was good.

The next site was in Hamilton, opposite the racecourse. We realised that we had the main central-belt population of Scotland covered, so the next step was England.

In quick succession we opened centres in Liverpool, Manchester, Sheffield and Newcastle. The centres didn't take off as quickly as we had anticipated. While all the Scottish centres were regularly full with what we would call 'casual' or 'pick-up' games, the English centres wanted leagues, competitive football.

03

The turf was worn down to the
concrete. There was a traffic cone
on the pitch. People had to play
around it!

We hadn't run leagues on that scale before so it was a learning curve, but we got to grips with it and continued to build the business up.

We were then approached to sell our company and 3I [a venture capitalist firm] was the winning bid. I was asked to stay on as the Chief Executive but I took the view that I could do better if I went away and started again.

The day the deal was done I handed in my letter of resignation and walked out the door.

Then you bought over another Glasgow-based 5-a-side business, Goals...

The family which owned Goals explained to me that it stood for Glasgow Open Air Leisure Services. I remember asking the owner if the name Goals came first or did Glasgow Open Air Leisure Services come first and then they realised it spelt 'Goals'! Joking aside, you couldn't get a more perfect name so we kept it.

There were five centres in total: Glasgow South, Glasgow West, Aberdeen, Wembley and Dagenham. In essence, the new business started with a blank sheet. From the very beginning we put in systems and processes, and started investing in IT to build a backbone that could handle a much bigger business. It was important to think ahead in what we were planning to do.

The first thing we did was travel to Holland and visit FC Twente **(left)** because I had heard that they had this new rubber crumb turf. I remember walking across the grass pitches and eventually I realised I was standing on a rubber crumb pitch. I had only ever experienced sand-filled pitches and immediately thought 'Wow, there is no going back. We have to have this'.

The Glasgow South centre was so badly run down when we bought it, there was a traffic cone on one of the pitches because there was a hole in the turf worn down to the concrete. People had to play football around the traffic cone! The week we bought Goals, the Environmental Health came in and threatened closure because it was a danger, so we had to re-turf the pitches – a perfect opportunity to use the new turf we had experienced in Holland

I remember watching the first set of games played on the 3G turf – people were slide-tackling and goalkeepers were diving for the ball. On a sand-filled pitch you were always aware of the playing surface and how it constantly affected the way you played. If you were a goalkeeper, for instance, you were wrapped up like the Michelin Man in case you ended up in Accident and Emergency. The great advantage of the 3G pitch was that you played the game, you didn't play the surface – that created a fundamental shift in the game.

The response to the 3G rubber crumb was incredibly positive. We followed suit and made changes to the other sites.

Goals as a new venture appeared to have a strong emphasis on the quality of the experience...

There are people who will get a ball and play 5-a-side on any surface or situation because they love the game so much, but I took the view that if we were going to attract a whole new player base into the game then a new approach was needed. I am talking about the guys who played football in school and stopped when they left because there were no other avenues to play. There was no recreational game. Or the recreational game was jumpers for goal posts. I thought there was an opportunity to get people in their 30s and 40s back into the game if you offered a quality facility for the recreational form of football.

To achieve this you had to create a facility to a much higher standard because this particular player base wasn't your 'diehard' who would play under any conditions. It was a player base who might have a negative perception of football – the idea of muddy pitches, bent goals posts and cold showers.

Life was changing for the better around that time and people's expectations had shifted. In order to capture a wider spectrum of the demographic we had to create something new.

You can play football to a very high standard and enjoy 5-a-side. Some of the 5-a-side teams we have could give the professionals a run for their money because the game requires a particular set of skills. Watching the top 5-a-side teams in the UK is like experiencing an art form. Conversely, you can be a bit on the heavy side but turn up and play with all your mates and still get the same enjoyment. An added bonus is that you will end up dropping a few stone over the course of the year, and getting much healthier. When you look at why people play football there are three top reasons – the love of the game, fitness and the social side of the sport.

So 5-a-side originates from the west of Scotland, a particularly obsessed football culture...

You're right. It is a cradle and the west of Scotland was the birth place of 5-a-side football, I believe. If you look at what is happening now, 5-a-side is turning into a global movement. The FA came out with a stat 10 years ago that stated 5-a-side football had caught up with 11-a-side football in participation. Last year [2014] the stats showed 5-a-side was twice as big. That is an incredible statistic when you think back to the days of kicking a ball around YMCA halls. It was a niche sport then and today it is twice as big as the national sport – in many ways it is the national sport!

The unique thing about 5-a-side is you can come into the game when you are five years old, because of the size of the pitch, and if you want to, and are good enough, then graduate to the 11-a-side game. There are people who play 11-a-side and who play 5-a-side as a form of training. Then there are people who are 30 and upwards who drop back down to play 5-a-side. There is a movement between the two games. The FA now embraces the 5-a-side game because they realise that it complements 11-a-side.

The participation levels in the sport and the expansion of your company suggests further potential for growth. How do you see the company developing?

I think the best is yet to come. Goals has huge potential as a company. I took the view that I should take the company to the United States – not Europe – for lots of different reasons. I believe America is on a path to adopting soccer as one of their national sports. The growth is massive and arguably it is the most popular participation team sport in the US.

In Californian schools, soccer, to use their terminology, has been one of the most popular participation sports for close to a decade now, so there's been loads of kids choosing to play soccer in high school. However, when they come out of high school there's nothing for them to move on to, unlike here in the UK where we are well provided for in terms

of grass pitches and full size all-weather pitches. In a city like LA, which has 18m people, finding a local park would be a miracle because the city is built up to an incredible degree. Also, after the kids leave high school there are other sports, the big three – baseball, American football and basketball – competing for their time. We have the first pilot site, in LA, and it is going well. You do not enter the American market just to open two or three sites – you do it for a reason. The opportunity is substantial. We are slowly building up the property and land banks required to open many centres. The professional game is also catching up with participation levels and you are seeing that reflected in the attendances at games in the MLS.

01   Keith Rogers

02   The old Portobello pool before its transformation into a Pitz soccer centre © Miles Cumming

03   A trip to the academy of Twente Enschede

in Holland persuaded Keith Rogers that the future of 5-a-side was 3G

04   Goals California. The centre in Los Angeles is the start of an ambitious drive into the USA

04

Turf Wars

We answer the big questions about artificial turf, the bedrock of the 5-a-side revolution. Is it better than grass? What's the difference between 3G and 4G? And what the hell are all these little black balls in my socks?

There are a generation of 5-a-side players – probably born before the mid-80s – who bear the physical scars of their early forays onto artificial turf. You'll see them on the beach in the summer, usually with permanently red knees or deep grazes where the dreaded sand-based 2G turf shredded them to the bone 20 years ago.

A mere mention of astroturf will still make them wince, transporting these victims back to their ill-fated encounters with the arse-shredding concrete carpets which prevailed in the 1980s and 90s.

The 2G surfaces were great for field hockey, but hopeless for football. They offered very little grip and it beggars belief that its popularity extended beyond 5-a-side. Queen's Park Rangers, Luton, Oldham Athletic and Preston North End all had 'plastic pitches' in the 1980s, before they were banned due to injuries and complaints about the standard of football.

Nowadays, artificial turf is a joy to play on. With its long, lush carpet features it's almost as good as real grass. Some would say it's even better. It plays evenly, doesn't wear into a mud bath and, after it has been installed, it's relatively maintenance free.

01   Terry Venables on QPR's 2G pitch

But artificial turf is still mysterious to some of us and there's a lot of confusing information out there about it.

G Force

No doubt you've heard the terms 3G and 4G bandied around. No, they're not different types of phone signal. They refer to 'third generation' and 'fourth generation' types of artificial turf. The general idea is that the more G, the more technological advancement it incorporates, and the closer your experience should resemble playing on real grass.

These days though, everyone is keen to offer you a little more 'G' than anyone else, with some claiming to have 5G, 6G, and even 7G turf. Very quickly, the descriptions of these surfaces are beginning to resemble bra-sizes, and it surely won't be long before someone is offering us 36GG.

The truth is, officially we haven't really got beyond 3G...

3G is the stuff that has a longer pile (the technical way of saying 'longer strands'), so it looks like actual blades of grass rather than the 2G sandpaper-carpet hybrid. These surfaces have sand and rubber-crumb spread all over it to improve the surface (they call this the 'infill'). They are also typically fitted with an underlying drainage system and some shock-absorbing underlay (to make them kinder on the joints).

Everyone wants to give you a little more 'G' – it won't be long before someone is offering 36GG

Why do people claim to have more than 3G?

Firstly, and most cynically, it's a sales-strategy. Who wants to be playing on 3G when they're being told that there's 4G, 5G or even 6G available? And since none of us know any better, we'll usually believe it.

But secondly, there are some manufacturers who believe that they may legitimately have developed 4G surfaces. Although there's no common agreement on what defines a 4G surface, the distinction that the manufacturers generally try to draw is that their versions of 4G surfaces are long-pile, but do not need any rubber infill.

The FA in their '3G Football Turf Guidance' (2012) said the following:

"At the moment there is no such thing as 4G or 5G, terms sometimes used by sales-people. Some manufacturers may promote non-infilled products, but these have not received acceptance as a suitable football surface and often struggle to satisfy FIFA requirements"

That was back in 2012, but there's still no sign that the FA or FIFA officially recognise any advancement on this. In 2015 the English FA announced it would continue a construction programme of 3G pitches across the UK.

What are those rubber bits you find on artificial turf?

This is called 'rubber crumb', and you'll find thousands of these little things on 3G playing surfaces.

Rubber crumb is recovered from tires (yes, the ones you have on your car) and has a number of other uses beyond covering football pitches: it's also used in road construction, for example.

James Dooley, of Soft Surfaces Ltd, explains why so many of these rubber crumb particles are used on artificial turf all over the world:

"These rubber infill particles help to keep the fake grass fibres upright and replicate natural playing characteristics of real grass. The rubber crumb can also help to cushion players' muscles and joints during training and matches to prevent injury and strain. It's important to keep a 3G fake grass pitch in top condition by regularly redistributing the rubber infill and topping it up if it becomes low. This will maintain good playing qualities and prevent the turf from becoming slippery."

Why do I get so many of these rubber bits in my shoes when I play?

There are few guarantees in 5-a-side football, but you can always be sure that at the end of a game you will have amassed a collection of little rubber bits stuck to your socks or inside your boots.

But exactly how many of these tiny rubber souvenirs are we taking home from football every week? We started emptying out or boots after each game and **below** is how much was picked up after just three one-hour games of 5-a-side.

Although it looks like a lot, our collection only weighs 6g. Given that a car tire weighs around 10kg, we're still roughly another 4,997 games away from collecting enough rubber bits to melt them back down and return them 'full-circle' to their former life as a car tire.

Are 3G Turf pitches safe?

In a word: yes. But that hasn't stopped a number of concerns being raised. The most common of these is the fear that players are more likely to get injured on artificial pitches than they are on grass.

In 2013, the Journal of Sports Medicine published a study looking at 1.5m hours of training and match play and almost 10,000 injuries. And after all that, they concluded that there was "no evidence that playing matches or training on artificial turf raises the risk of soccer players sustaining injury".

In fact, the evidence suggested that the risks of some types of injuries might even be lowered.

The second safety fear has been around whether the rubber-crumb might be harmful, particularly to young children. The US Environmental Agency did a limited study across a small number of facilities and concluded that the limited data they collected did not point to a concern. Assuming that you're not eating rubber-crumb (it makes a very poor salad-sprinkle) the evidence suggests you'll be fine.

1. Good 3G pitches play like natural grass, before it gets all worn and patchy.

2. Research has shown that there is no increased risk of injury on artificial grass.

3. Because these surfaces offer a consistent roll and bounce of the ball all over the pitch, 3G pitches encourage technically better play than grass.

4. 3G surfaces are playable in a lot more weather conditions resulting in little, if any postponements.

Is artificial turf better than natural grass?

This is a very emotive issue, and the answer often depends on who you ask. If you could guarantee top-notch grass surfaces every single time, then the majority of people would opt for natural grass. But as anybody who has been down to their local grass football field knows, it's incredibly rare to find grass in perfect condition and, more often than not you're looking at an uneven, patchy quagmire instead; the sort of surface that's more suited for grazing cattle than trying to play the beautiful game.

'Fans for 3G', a movement that aims to get full-sized 3G pitches into professional clubs, has passionately set out the following reasons (which we summarised) on why the gospel of artificial pitches should be spread throughout the land:

And of course, one of the coolest things about artificial grass 5-a-side pitches is that they now come in all sorts of incredible colours. And you can't get that effect with natural grass, unless you're on hallucinogenic drugs...

What footwear should I wear for artificial turf?

If it's 3G, rubber-crumb surface, you have a choice of what you can wear. This ranges from special astroturf trainers, to moulded (hard-ground) boots, and now special 'AG' ('artificial grass') boots which are somewhere between the two. Long-studded 'soft-ground' boots and blades are best left for playing on grass.

Tales from the pitch

A nose for goal

by Alex Pringle

Many years ago, I played in a 5-a-side game which was, let's say, attritional in nature. It wasn't so much physically violent as populated with several moaners who should have been concentrating on their own deficiencies rather than constantly pointing out other people's. Anyway, one regular barely uttered a word throughout these weekly encounters. This guy had two speeds: 'Stop' and 'Go'. He rarely marked his man – for which the 'moaners' endlessly heckled him – but was capable of speedy bursts and some decent finishing.

I never once saw him make a tackle. Until this one day. His big trick was to drop a shoulder then go the opposite way. Only this time it didn't work. He dropped a shoulder, went the other way – but the defender held his ground. In an attempt to force his way past, the speedy winger threw up his arm, smashing his forearm into the defender's face. The guy went down like a giant oak. Geysers of blood spurted over the green turf. Broken nose. Luckily, the Accident and Emergency ward of the local hospital was just across a footbridge adjacent to the park. So, holding his nose in place, the defender wandered over the bridge – still in his shorts and t-shirt – to get patched up. We played on with nine men.

Ten minutes later, identical scenario. The speedy winger drops a shoulder, it doesn't work and he smashes another opponent across the nose. Another torrent of blood. Another player making the lonely walk across the footbridge.

"You never make a tackle in 20 years and suddenly you've claimed two bodies in 10 minutes," someone said to the speedy winger. He didn't reply, though he did have the good grace to look a little sheepish.

The 5-a-side Pioneer

When Britain was swinging in the 1960s, Glyn Ward was organising fives tournaments. He fought for FA recognition and laid the foundation for the explosion of the small-sided game that would follow

In 1969 Glyn Ward volunteered to run a 5-a-side tournament at the County Day festival in Hertfordshire. It went well – there were crowds eight-deep watching the action and plenty of teams wanting to take part. Glyn was on to something.

That summer, he was granted clearance from the FA to form the Ware and District 5-a-side League, the first organised adult 5-a-side league in the area, and one of the first nationwide. Glyn's leagues went on to become legendary in that part of the world across four decades. He was an organiser, he was a referee, he was a champion for the power of 5-a-side football – and that he remains.

We caught up with Glyn to talk about being a 5-a-side pioneer – and to focus on the unique demands faced by referees in 5-a-side.

How did your first league start up?
It was held over 12 weeks in the summer – I was a PE teacher, but this was my hobby. In our first year, in 1969, there were 33 teams in the league across three divisions, but it soon started to grow. We added a fourth division in 1972, a fifth division in 1973, and a sixth division in 1978.

The league was played entirely on grass for the first few years, anywhere we could find a venue. We even played at the local boys' home. We had two pitches put in there so they could play because they weren't allowed to leave the site!

I got 5-a-side goals made through my contacts, who were welders and in the building trade. They welded scaffolding poles together for goals, which were bloody heavy! I got my students to carry them up to the venue in their PE lesson.

At its peak the league was nine divisions of 11 teams. I organised most of it single-handedly, without computers. It was hard work and I lost count of the hours I spent doing it, but I did it because I loved it. Some of the guys who played in the leagues used to tell me that I'd saved their lives organising all this football. Playing for those 12 weeks in the summer kept them out of mischief.

You spent years refereeing these games – what's that like?

I have refereed 11-a-side games and 5-a-side is physically less demanding for a referee, especially when the pitch is enclosed. Your vision is better and you're near the action all the time.

We used to affiliate our league to the FA and all the players had to be registered. We did this because it helped us enforce discipline. In the early 2000s we were giving the FA so much work – during what should have been their quiet months – that they told us to set up our own internal fines system and keep the money! We had 300 matches going on each week – teams played three games per week – and you could have up to 100 cautions being referred to them. So we held a meeting and brought in our own system, and we made in the region of £1000 a year in fines, which helped keep the fees down. We still passed serious instances, like headbutts, punches and violent conduct to the FA.

One of the problems in some leagues is that the players don't seem to fear discipline because there are very seldom any consequences. A lot of times a player will be sent off on the night but it doesn't go any further. No fines, no suspensions. Only if it's serious does it go further. One time we had a goalkeeper run the entire length of the pitch to punch the referee. We banned him for life.

What makes people lose it on the pitch?

Some of the nicest blokes off the pitch are bad on the pitch. It's the competition. A lot of them can't condition themselves to go from 11-a-side, which is physical with slide-tackles, body-checks and contact, to 5-a-side, which is minimal body contact with no slides, no studs up.

It's the enclosed space as well. The proximity of the ball and the players to the sides results in ankle-taps, niggly things, kicks in the backs of legs, reactions using elbows.

The rules can vary from game to game – what was your experience of that?

We were innovators, we brought in dotted areas a few feet around the usual one, and fouls inside were penalties – we had to ask the FA for that. We also petitioned the FA for the use of sin-bins for 10 years before they let us use them.

One year the FA told us that we had to get rid of the head-height rule and the area rule. I am in favour of the head-height rule because it seems to result in more controlled football. Some of the good players score some wonderful goals without it, but a lot of people didn't like that the goalkeeper could just slam the ball down the field and it spoiled the passing game.

I would also have the area rule as it protects the goalkeeper. But I would allow the goalkeeper out of the area as then it's a lot more like basketball and you see some great play. You can come out of the area in 11-a-side, why not in 5-a-side?

What makes a good referee?

Good referees control the game from the start. When a bad tackle is not penalised, somebody else retaliates.

You need to have been a player to be a good referee. You know the game and you know when somebody goes in on purpose, and what creates aggravation. You also know when somebody is cheating.

Players don't like being penalised. They never think they're wrong and will argue about fouls, throw-ins, even silly things.

When did it cross the line?

I was once refereeing a game where somebody elbowed an opponent in the face. It was behind my back so I didn't see who had done it, but I knew who it was. The next week this lad's dad came up to 5-a-side with him demanding to know who did it. Frankly, they should have got the police involved, it was assault.

We once had a guy from New Zealand refereeing for us. He was refereeing a game where someone else assaulted another player. He went to get the offender's name and was told to fuck off. But this referee was a policeman. He got his police ID out and said 'right, I'm going to have you for assault'. The player ran off, but the ref later went round to his house and charged him for it. He never refereed again after that; he said he was finding it too difficult to separate the refereeing and his job as a policeman!

15 Players
You Always See
At 5-a-side

We all like to think we're unique players, bringing our individual styles and dominant personalities to bear during our weekly kickabouts. We're not. Chances are you know one of these guys – or you are one...

The Organiser

Explanation: Sender of the weekly group text. Has a credit account with the local park. His little black book would put Russell Brand to shame. Never forgives a late call-off. Would get a game on in the immediate aftermath of a zombie apocalypse.

Pro equivalent: Gary Neville

Most likely to say: "We're a man down – I know your broken leg hasn't fully healed, but you wouldn't leave the boys in the lurch, would you?"

Least likely to say: "You look a bit under the weather mate, why don't you just give it a miss tonight. We'll be fine with nine."

The Latecomer

Explanation: Lost his watch in 1991, never replaced it. His warm-up is the sprint from the car park to the pitch where his mates have already kicked off with nine. Throws his keys and phone behind the net and doesn't even have the decency to go in goals first.

Pro equivalent: Andrei Arshavin

Most likely to say: "Traffic was murder, lads. Right, who's in my team?"

Least likely to say: "What time do you call this?"

The Moaner

Explanation: The volume of his rants are inversely proportionate to his talent. Uses the weekly game as a perverse kind of therapy, finding a release for his frustrations over a failing marriage, expanding waistline and career cul-de-sac in a bitter tirade against both team-mates and opponents.

Pro: Roy Keane

Most likely to say: "Mark up! Track back! Goal side! Show him onto his left! Don't dive in! Hit him!"

Least likely to say: "Sorry lads that was my fault."

The Veteran

Explanation: Oldest player on the pitch. Always at the back. Played 11s at a good level. Knows all the tricks on both sides of the law. Reads the game like Beckenbauer. Most vulnerable in the last 20 minutes, when he employs the dark arts to stay on top of the whippersnappers.

Pro equivalent: Franco Baresi

Most likely to say: "MARK UP!"

Least likely to say: "Take the foot off the gas, lads. This is in the bag."

The Step-over King

Explanation: Spends the warm-up doing keepie-uppies by himself with the only ball you have, wearing fluorescent trainers. Opponents soon work out his repertoire of FIFA tricks. This show pony never tracks back and wonders why he always ends up on the losing team.

Pro equivalent: Denilson

Most likely to say: "If that third rabona had come off we'd have won."

Least likely to say: "Nothing beats the five-yard pass."

The Big Man

Explanation: Nice touch for a big man. Overweight, under-estimated. Foot like a pillow, turning circle like a JCB. Can trap a speeding bullet. Just don't ask him to track back.

Pro equivalent: Jan Molby

Most likely to say: "Play it to my feet."

Least likely to say: "Who's up for some warm-down sprints?"

The Goal Hanger

Explanation: Knows where the goal is – because he never strays more than two metres from it. Keeps an audible running tally of his goals – will aggressively argue that his goalscoring stats outweigh the refusal to defend which has led to a narrow defeat for his team.

Pro equivalent: Pippo Inzaghi

Most likely to say: "Why didn't you just pass to me?"

Least likely to say: "There's no 'i' in team."

The Shooter

Explanation: Yes, he does have a good shot. But he's more Rambo than American Sniper, spraying the back wall with wayward piledrivers while ignoring team-mates in better positions. Responsible for ball-marked thighs, bruised testicles and the occasional concussion. Never apologises.

Pro equivalent: Thomas 'The Hammer' Hitzlsperger

Most likely to say: "Have it!"

Least likely to say: "Sorry, I should have squared it."

The Assassin

Explanation: Early 40s, just a little bit overweight. Wife-beater vest displaying old-school arm ink. Footwear custom-built for maximum damage. The boards are his partner in crime and he'll slam you into them like he's an ice hockey enforcer. Slide tackles on any surface. May once have killed a man.

Pro equivalent: Vinnie Jones

Most likely to say: "It's a man's game, son."

Least likely to say: "Take it easy, it's only a kickabout."

The Crock

Explanation: Always injured. Or coming back from an injury. Or petrified of picking up another injury. Knee strap. Ankle support. Knows more about the human body than a Harley Street doctor. Diagnoses on-pitch injuries in real-time – usually wrongly.

Pro equivalent: Jack Wilshere

Most likely to say: "That looks like a grade one tear of the adductor muscle, mate."

Least likely to say: "It's cool. I'll run it off…"

Cinderella

Explanation: Always leaves on the stroke of full-time, as if staying a second over will see him turn into a pumpkin. Scores are level, it's end-to-end action, the best game for weeks. As you look to your left for a pass, you see him zipping up his top and scurrying off into the night without a word, oblivious to the murderous glares from team-mates and opponents.

Most likely to say: "Sorry, lads – need to get home for the start of Gogglebox."

Least likely to say: "Let's play till they chuck us off."

The Weakest Link

Explanation: Worst player by a country mile. Usually a nice guy, which makes it impossible to dish out the bollocking he deserves on a weekly basis. Team-mates fall into a damaging cycle of negative reinforcement, where the merest display of competence is cheered as if it was the winning goal in the World Cup final.

Pro equivalent: David May

Most likely to say: "Sorry."

Least likely to say: "Give it me and I'll do the rest."

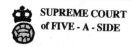

The Net Dodger

Explanation: Will do anything to avoid his turn in goal. Prone to lingering at the other end of the field and avoiding eye contact with his team-mates when it's his turn. Will not accept that it's his turn until issued with court papers and frogmarched to the 'D'. Lets in a soft goal almost immediately to get back out again.

Most likely to say: "I've been in twice already."

Least likely to say: "I'll stay in for another."

The Full-Kit Wanker

Explanation: Kitted out head to toe in this season's strip. Socks pulled right up, sponsors' logo stretched across his ample midriff, name of his team's captain on the back and donning the footwear endorsed by the skipper. Always the worst player in the game.

Pro equivalent: John Terry

Most likely to say: "I feel proud to pull this jersey over my head every week."

Least likely to say: "This is last year's kit. Couldn't afford the new one."

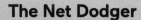

The Human Scoreboard

Explanation: Annoys everyone with his endless scorekeeping. Most vocal when his team are in front, but strangely silent when they are on the wrong end of a skelping. Prone to creative accounting, particularly when his team are behind, at which point a four-goal deficit can vanish in an instant.

Most likely to say: "That's one / two / three to us."

Least likely to say: "That's one / two / three to you."

Zola
v
Courtois

5-a-side
Dream Team

Our Verdict – Zola win

This could be a massacre. Falcao gets no change out of Maldini and Desailly, and Maradona destroys Filipe Luís

Gianluigi Buffon

Paolo Maldini **Marcel Desailly**

Roberto Di Matteo

Diego Maradona

Source: theFA.com

Source: Chelseafc.com

Koke **Radamel Falcao**

Eden Hazard

Filipe Luís

Thibaut Courtois

Legends of 5-a-side

The Greatest

Sofiane Ferrad, 'Sof' for short, is the man widely regarded to have single-handedly transformed the UK fives scene. His mercurial talent has set the benchmark for all who now play the game

He might not have appeared on Sky Sports every weekend, but ask any serious 5-a-side player who has seen him play and they will tell you Sof's influence on amateur footballers around the country runs much deeper than that of the vast majority of pros.

Quite simply, Sof has been a one-man revolution. Trail-blazing his way through the 5-a-side scene, even now, in his late 40s, he's still making a mockery of defenders. Like the Frank Sinatra of 5-a-side, any connoisseur knows at least a few of his greatest hits, and what's more: he did it his way.

From being done-and-dusted with football altogether, to winning more 5-a-side trophies than he's got space for in his house: this is the legend of Sof.

Tell us about your background...
I was born in 1969 in Algeria. I used to go to France a lot because I have a big family there in Marseille. There is a big Algerian community in France – famous names such as Zidane, Nasri and Benzema are all of Algerian descent.

In Algeria, we used to play outside in the street. During breaks at school, we'd go outside and play football on the concrete. Playing on concrete so much is what later hurt my knees but that's where I learned my tricks, playing for hours in the street. Back in those days we didn't have mobile phones. People would come and knock at the door, leaving messages with my mum that I was needed for big games happening in the town.

on. I couldn't even speak English back in those days but a referee knew me and one day he asked me if I wanted a game. From that one game, people wanted me to play more, and that's when I consider that my life in England really started.

Once I learned the game nobody could stop me. Even Raheem Sterling watched me when he was young

I played for the reserve team in Marseille in the 1990s, when they had a very good team. I didn't really play with any of the first-team players, though. I used to be a bad boy and when I got a serious knee injury the club didn't want to know, so I just started trying to get on with my life outside of football. But if you're not playing football you get a little bit down, and you get into the wrong things. So I went back to Algeria.

And then you moved to England and found 5-a-side...
I decided to come to England in 1997 and lived near Alperton, in London, which had a 5-a-side centre. After work I used to go down there just to watch what was going

Each time I played against someone, they would take my number and give me a call asking me to be on their team. At one point I used to play three times a night, five days a week. My knees suddenly felt fine for the first time in years and I was managing to play 15 games a week – it was unbelievable, especially as I thought my football was behind me.

I had never seen this format of 5-a-side before. Even when I had played in France, they didn't use the rule where you can't go in the area. So when I first started playing, I struggled – always running inside the area and giving away free-kicks. But when I started to learn the game, nobody could stop me.

You have your own distinctive style. How did you create your own 5-a-side game?

The way I play, it's my way of playing, not something I copied from somebody else. If I want to do a trick, I am determined to learn it. Even if it goes wrong the first few times and people start laughing, I become even more determined to get it right. That's what I tell the younger guys – if you want to do a trick, just do it; don't panic. If people are laughing at you, don't worry about it – just think about the next time, and getting better.

I have a famous drag-back that I created; nobody else taught me it. A lot of the 5-a-side players use that trick for themselves these days. So many people have watched me play over the years – even Raheem Sterling used to watch me playing when he was young.

What's your preferred position?

I play as a pivot [the attacker]. I'm not a big guy but I know how to use my body. When I receive the ball I have my back to the defender, and then the defender can't see the ball, so I can deceive him with a trick.

I play using the bottom of my foot a lot. That's because on a 5-a-side pitch there's not a lot of space and you need to be able to hold the ball with your sole. You have to be able to think quickly too; use your brain. Before the ball gets to you, have an idea of what you're going to do with it. Think about whether you're going to dribble right or left.

SOF's 5–a–side masterclass

What makes a good 5-a-side player?

Determination – I always try hard. You need to play with your heart. Not just for fun, not just because you fancy a trip out of your house; play from the heart.

Prepare properly for a game. I always arrive early for a game, sometimes 30 minutes before the start; then I go to the changing room, change properly, put my shin pads and my shirt on, then I go out and watch the game before us. If I can, I warm up so that by the time the game starts I am mentally ready.

When you're training try putting 10 cones in a row. Then dribble in and out of the cones making sure that you don't touch them. Make sure that you use big cones (rather than the small floor-markers that you can just easily step over) because they force you to improve your balance ducking in and out of them. I used to do this as a kid and I think that it's one of the big reasons that I have such good balance today.

I attack them on their weaker foot when I can.

How successful have you been?

Since 1997 I have probably won more than 900 trophies. I've got them all at home! My brother put a cabinet in my sitting room and I've put the best ones in there. But the others are all in boxes; I don't want to throw them away because I had to work hard for them. Some of the trophies are for winning big tournament, but really they're all special.

In 2004, I tried my best to count how many goals I scored in that whole year – this was when I was playing about 15 games a week – and I reckon I scored more than 1,000. People are playing a bit more defensively these days, especially when it's tournament football – teams are looking to go one goal up and then just defend.

How does it feel to be a role model to so many 5-a-side players?

I'm proud of the fact that my name is always talked about wherever there's 5-a-side. I like to try to be a model for the younger players. I've had people wanting photos with me. I've even had a couple of people ask for an autograph!

It is amazing to think that all this has happened just through playing 5-a-side. When I think back to when I first came to England, I thought I was done with football and I was at a low. 5-a-side has changed my life.

The Secrets of Sof

Drag back – standing side-on to the defender, who will be between you and the goal, roll the ball backwards as if you are about to backheel it. As the defender moves in the direction you've dragged the ball, roll it forwards to create the vital space to get a shot off.

Spoon – make contact with the ball with the instep of your foot and start to push it forwards. In one movement, move your foot around the side of the ball and scoop it across your body. This unexpected change of direction will unbalance the defender.

Backheel – I use the backheel for scoring goals. I won so many important games with this technique. It comes from nowhere – the goalkeeper and the defender are behind you and it catches them completely by surprise.

Receiving a roll-out – to create some space for myself, I run one way and then quickly cut the other, which gives you a few steps head-start on a defender.

Toe-punts – Some people say that the toe-punt isn't a proper technique, but it works. It often catches a keeper by surprise.

What's the secret to playing for as long as possible?

I am currently 46 years old. I've managed to play for a long time because I have looked after myself. I don't eat McDonalds, I cook healthy things: salads, Mediterranean food, Italian. I use seasoning very carefully, I don't eat sugar, and I try to cut out salt. I drink water.

I don't know how long I will play for, but I've always said that when my body is tired I will call it a day. But I'm still feeling good.

5-a-side is a great release. Sometimes when I've got problems, I just love to go and play football. When you're playing football you forget everything that's going on outside of the pitch.

I'm proud of the fact that my name is always talked about wherever there's 5-a-side

01   With Sir Bobby Charlton

02   Sof photobombs Alan Shearer

03   Sky Sports News hails King Sof

04   With Ray Parlour

05   Alex Oxlade-Chamberlain, Sof and Danny Welbeck – not a bad front three

Tales from the pitch

Sing when you're losing

by Jason Stubbs

The worst 5-a-side team I ever played for were called Bayreuth. They played in the Saturday morning league in an area of Glasgow where Buckfast was the official drinks sponsor. I'm not saying it was rough, but the area was twinned with Baghdad – and the Iraqi city felt they got a bum deal.

I was asked to play by a friend of a friend of a friend. I feel three degrees of separation is just about enough to exonerate me from any responsibility. Initially, I thought they were called 'Beirut' then 'Babe Ruth' (perhaps they were big baseball fans, I mused) until I saw their name written down on the noticeboard at the venue. Bayreuth. As in, the German town with the famous opera house… no, I didn't get it either. You see, Bayreuth were composed of opera singers based at Glasgow's Royal Academy of Scottish Music and Drama.

Now, it's not that Bayreuth were really bad – they were pretty poor, but not embarrassingly so. It's just that they had no idea how to play competitive 5-a-side. In a league where only the streetwise survived, Bayreuth were quietly murdered every week.

We did win one game. It was against the second-bottom team in the league. I drafted in my cousin to help us out. We won 10-9, with my cousin scoring a last-minute winner. We both scored five goals apiece. The boys were ecstatic. The organiser of the team even took us to the Bon Accord pub for lunch and drinks. Myself and my cousin were so shattered that we had to phone his wife to come and pick us up from the pub.

I would say it was demoralising but I loved it. They were brilliant lads – polite, friendly, interesting, well educated, articulate… and they took all these laudable human qualities onto the roughest pitches in Glasgow every Saturday morning. It was like dropping kittens into the Savannah.

Then, one week, the game erupted in what the Daily Star might term "an orgy of violence". Our centre-forward – an impressive baritone with a voice that could shake the ornaments off the mantelpiece – called off sick, but arranged for his mate to play. His mate happened to be a French horn player.

In the roughest part of Glasgow the sending-off record is still held by a psychotic French horn player

After 10 minutes, he got into an argument with the ref over something innocuous. The ref sent him off. He stomped off and, just as he got to the door, returned to deliver another volley of abuse. He was shown a second red. Then, as he left the park again, he slammed the door so hard that it broke off its hinges. He was sent off a third time. In the roughest league in the roughest part of Glasgow, the sending-off record is still held by a psychotic French horn player.

It didn't end there. Near the end, one of their players slid in on our keeper, a chubby English tenor called Colin. Colin pushed him away, but the player grabbed him by the throat. All hell broke loose as Colin set about re-arranging the guy's face. It took three of us to pull him off.

"What the hell happened to Colin?" I asked afterwards. "I've never seen him react like that."

"Ah, it was because the guy grabbed him by the throat. He's an opera singer, right? So, his voice is the tool of his trade. If he loses that, he's finished."

There's a couple of morals to this tale. Firstly, never, ever grab an opera singer by the throat. Secondly, and more importantly, winning is irrelevant if you like your team-mates.

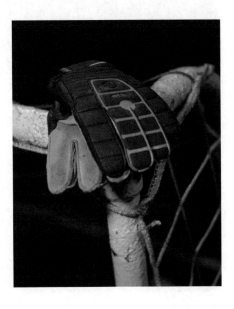

The Warm-up

"One part of my job I'll never learn to love is the pre-match warm-up. I hate it with every fibre of my being. It actually disgusts me. It's nothing but masturbation for conditioning coaches." Andrea Pirlo

Andrea Pirlo – "I hate the pre-match warm-up with every fibre of my being."

The vast majority of 5-a-side players take the Andrea Pirlo approach to warm-ups.

If there is a warm-up, it will often consist of a couple of players standing around firing balls at the goalkeeper (or whoever is daft enough to be standing in goal at the time), stopping occasionally to do some sort of on-the-spot stretch that they think might help their dodgy Achilles / hamstring / calf. And that's one of the more impressive warm-ups you'll see.

If your warm-up sounds like this, you're doing it wrong. That's a risk you don't want to take. Playing 5-a-side without performing a warm-up is going to significantly increase your chances of getting injured and ultimately reduce your playing time.

Why warm up?
Apart from the fact that it helps decrease injury, a warm-up also:

> **Prepares your body for exercise** – gradually raising your heart rate to the required level so that your first sprint after the ball isn't such a shock to the system

> **Mentally prepares you for the game** – it gives you a chance to focus on the game ahead and ensure that you're mentally ready

> **Increases power, agility and performance** – by getting the muscles warm and also by refreshing the link between brain and body, you're fully prepared and ready to perform to your best

THE EASY WARM-UP PLAN:

Your warm-up needn't be complicated - use this simple, scientifically developed routine

1. JOGGING

Jog straight ahead at a gentle pace (2 x 20m)

2. ROTATE HIP OUT

Jog a couple of paces. Stop. Lift your knee forwards; rotate it out to the side; then put your foot down.

Jog a couple more paces. Repeat on other leg. (5 on each leg)

3. ROTATE HIP IN

Jog a couple of paces. Stop. Lift your knee out to the side; rotate it inwards so it points forwards; then put your foot down.

Jog a couple more paces. Repeat on other leg. (5 on each leg)

Stay nice and light on your toes - don't strain anything

5. JUMPS

Jog a couple of paces. Stop and perform a standing jump (launching off both feet).

Jog a couple more paces forward and repeat (x 10)

Don't let your knees buckle as you land

4. SIDESTEPS

Jog a couple of paces. Stop. Sidestep 3 or 4 paces to the left. Then, sidestep the same number of paces to the right, back to your original path.

Jog forward and repeat (x 5)

6. FORWARDS &BACK

Run quickly forward for 10m. Then run backwards 5m.

Repeat x 10

7. 75-80% PACE

Run 40m at 75-80% pace.

Gently jog back and repeat one more time

Focus on the game ahead; prepare your mind

9. CHANGE DIRECTION

Run in a zig-zag. Sprint for 5-7 steps at 80-90% of maximum speed. Decelerate and plant your left leg, cutting to the right. Again, sprint forward to your right, decelerate and cut to your left.

8. BOUNDING

Take a few gentle paces then do 6-8 bounding steps - lifting your knee high, swinging the opposite arm across your body.

Jog back and repeat one more time

10. BALL-WORK

- ○ Dribbling: left foot, right foot. Instep, outside, sole
- ○ Passing and receiving: left foot, right foot. Instep, outside, sole
- ○ Shooting
- ○ Keepy-uppy (coordination)

Pick a few things from this list to focus on.

Reherse the things you know you need for the game

Dynamic stretches good, static stretches bad

Times have moved on. The classic warm-up, which 10 years ago consisted of some jogging followed by some static stretching, is rapidly being consigned to history.

Sports science is now telling us that a warm-up need not consist of any **static stretching** at all. A static stretch, in case you were wondering, is a stretch that you do whilst you're at rest. Static stretches were the core of the old-school warm-ups where you'd all stand around in a circle following somebody who would generally make up the stretches as he went along.

Research now seems to be showing that this type of static stretching makes you slower, and may actually increase your risk of injury.

Instead, **dynamic stretches** have taken over as the focus of a warm-up routine. They essentially involve stretching whilst performing gentle movements.

What exercises should I do?

There are lots of different ways to warm-up, but the way we recommend is using the exercises that have been supplied by FIFA's own sport's science department, which is contained in a programme it calls the 11. These are really straightforward exercises that are easily explained and executed.

The exercises consist of jogging, interspersed with movements that stretch specific muscle groups. Over the course of nine exercises, the intensity of the exercises increase until you are ready to unleash by the time kick-off comes around.

Everything you need to know has been condensed for your convenience into the infographic on page 72.

You can find videos of all of the exercises referenced in the infographic on the **FIFA 11 website**

It's really important that you perform these exercises with correct form – which means having your body in line and not allowing your knees to buckle. If you have any doubts on how to perform any of the exercises, it's worth watching the videos on the FIFA site.

Most importantly, through the warm-up, make sure that you **stay light on your toes** – don't strain anything. There is nothing more frustrating than injuring yourself before you have even kicked a ball.

Tips for success

Practically, there are a few common pitfalls that people tend to make when trying to do a warm-up. Here are some to avoid:

DO make sure that you leave enough time to warm-up before the game. This means arriving at the venue in advance of kick-off. If the pitch is full, warm-up by the side.

DO NOT start smashing the ball around before warming up, tempting as it is. This accounts for a huge number of injuries where people have pulled hamstrings or twisted ankles because they have overdone it with the ball without warming up first. In our warm-up plan the ball work doesn't start until you are warmed up.

DO make the routine fit you – if you need to do more of any particular exercise, then do it. However, watch out when adding static stretches and please never do the exercise where you try to touch your toes from a standing position – it's an injury waiting to happen.

DO NOT perform any stretches to the point of pain and do not hold your breath when stretching. Listen to your body; stop if it hurts.

Getting in the zone:
The Mental Warm-Up

"Some people don't understand how important it is to stretch your mind as well as your body before a match. The two need to be working together if you want to start a game well"
Fabrice Muamba

The need to perform a physical warm-up is well understood, but the majority of players don't consider doing a mental warm-up as part of their pre-game preparation. Without warming up your mind, your performance might not reach peak levels.

Go mental

If you're not warming up your mind for football then you're missing out on a whole host of potential benefits, which include:

An increased rate of neuromuscular transmission and recruitment of muscle fibres – or in other words, getting your muscles to listen and process the signals that they're going to be getting from the control centre: your brain activating "neuromuscular memory" for the event's specific movements – get your brain to remind your body how good it is at football. This stops you making a sloppy start to the match.

It doesn't have to be difficult

The good news is that you don't need to choose between a physical warm-up and a mental warm-up, as the two can be done at the same time.

Nor does a mental warm-up need to be complex. It can be as simple as taking a few moments to yourself before the game and concentrating on the following:

Focus on how the ball feels at your feet – is it moving how you want it to? Are you controlling a pass as well as you know you can? If not, repeat key movements until you've calibrated your brain (and the techniques and movements it drives) to accommodate the surface and conditions.

Think about the things that you can do in the game to make sure that you perform most effectively. Practice any specific movements that are needed for these things – perform them with confidence.

As kick-off approaches, ask yourself if you feel as though you've reached game intensity in your warm-up. The final stages of the warm-up should bring your mind in tune with your body and make sure that both are up to 100% game intensity.

Most 5-a-side players will know little about the opposition and, most of the time, that's all that is needed. Don't spend your time worrying too much about the opposition players.

Instead, focus on what *you* control: your own performance.

Winners think positive thoughts before the game. Focus on your game and the things that you know you can do well – envisage yourself doing them.

Professionals understand this better than the amateur players. That might be because they've had more time working with sports psychologists, or maybe they always had that attitude and that's what took them to the top. Either way, the importance of warming up your mind for football is something that players of every level can benefit from.

Cooling Down

(How a bit of stretching can up your game)

It's game over. But you're not finished yet. The pub can wait – a few simple stretches now will give you benefits you haven't even imagined

'THAT'S TIME!'

The shout breaks the spell of the game just as your team have got it back to 'one down'. By the time you turn to see where it came from, the next game is streaming through the gate in the corner of the pitch. You know the rules. You now have about 20 seconds to shake hands with your mates, gather up your hoodie, car keys and phone, and get out of Dodge.

You have as much chance of going through a cool-down (or warm-down) as you have of persuading the 10 players preparing to start their game that they should let you play an extra five minutes.

What now? A few minutes of stretching would aid recovery and injury prevention. You're still in your kit.

Instead you limp to your car. Or stand around in the cold, talking about what went wrong. Or head for the bar.

This is how the game ends for the vast majority of players. So what are we all missing out on? We spoke to **Craig Ball (right)**, a personal trainer and an expert in the benefits of post-exercise activity. He explained why a good cool-down is as important a part of your game as your signature step-over, or that no-look inside pass you're so fond of.

Heart rate, repair and flexibility
Craig: The goal of your cool-down is to help ease the body back into its pre-exercise state. With the high intensity nature of 5-a-side, your **heart rate** will likely be very high; this needs to be brought down gradually, rather than going from all-out maximum effort to a complete stand-still. Lowering your heart rate too quickly can lead to sudden dizziness as your body struggles to move from an intense work-out to almost total rest.

Having a gradual cool-down encourages the blood to keep circulating around your body – a vital part of optimal **body repair**. Blood is used to carry nutrients and oxygen to the parts of your body that need them most. During a tough game, your body is subject to stresses and strains. By the end it is sore and a little damaged. You need to help the repair job in any way you can.

A cool-down can also help your **flexibility**. After the game, your muscles are very warm, which is an ideal state for stretching. Stretching regularly allows your muscles to be lengthened, leading to a greater range of motion – something you'll be wishing you had the next time you strain yourself stretching to make a tackle.

If you've been banished from the pitch and space is an issue, jogging on the spot is fine

A simple cool-down routine

Craig: Between five and 10 minutes of easy exercise after a game will help with the gradual lowering of the heart rate. If you've been banished from the pitch and space is an issue, **jogging on the spot** is fine. Start at a higher pace and gradually slow it down over the duration. Some deep breathing to help oxygenate your system is also encouraged.

Following this, your body is ready for some **static stretching**. A static stretch is where you hold a stretch in one position without any movement. It's the opposite of a **dynamic stretch**, where you do move as you stretch – a method that is more appropriately used in a pre-match warm-up.

The more areas of your body you can stretch the better, but you should heavily focus on the *legs and lower back* as it's these that are most important for football.

As a minimum, try doing the following **5 simple stretches** after you play. It's best if you can maintain each stretch for 20-30 seconds per muscle group. If you know what you're doing you'll be done with all five in around two minutes – less time than you usually spend arguing about who was at fault for the final goal.

GROIN

- STAND WITH LEGS WIDER THAN SHOULDER WIDTH APART
- SHIFT WEIGHT ON TO ONE SIDE AND BEND KNEE
- REACH ONE HAND TOWARDS OUTSTRETCHED FOOT

HAMSTRINGS

- LIFT TOE AND PUT HANDS ON KNEE OF LEG TO BE STRETCHED
- LOWER YOUR UPPER BODY, KEEPING YOUR BACK STRAIGHT & LEG STRAIGHT UNTIL YOU FEEL THE STRETCH IN YOUR HAMSTRING

QUADRICEPS

- STAND ON ONE LEG AND GRAB FOOT, PULLING THE HEEL INTO YOUR BUTTOCKS
- YOUR BENT KNEE SHOULD STAY PARALELL WITH STANDING LEG
- PUSH HIPS OUT TO INCREASE STRETCH

CALF

- USE WALL / FENCE TO SUPPORT YOU, PLACE ONE LEG STRETCHED BEHIND YOU
- KEEPING OTHER LEG BENT, LEAN FORWARDS TO APPLY PRESSURE TO BACK LEG.
- KEEP BACK HEEL FLAT ON GROUND

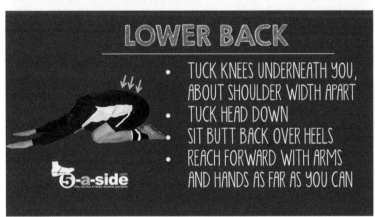

LOWER BACK

- TUCK KNEES UNDERNEATH YOU, ABOUT SHOULDER WIDTH APART
- TUCK HEAD DOWN
- SIT BUTT BACK OVER HEELS
- REACH FORWARD WITH ARMS AND HANDS AS FAR AS YOU CAN

That final stretch? I know, you're thinking: 'No way, I've never seen anybody do that after a game of football.'

The first four stretches were selected because they are ones that you can do standing up on a wet or dirty surface. Unfortunately lower back stretches just don't come like that. Don't skip it – a good lower back stretch will be really appreciated by your hamstrings! If anybody asks what you're doing, just casually say that you're offering prayers to the gods of 5-a-side.

Stretching helps develop flexibility and keeps muscles at their optimal length

What a cool-down will not do
A lot of people think that the main purpose of performing a cool-down is to stop you aching after a game. The theory goes that these routines will remove a build-up of lactic acid from the muscles which will lead to reduced aching.

Sadly, that particular theory isn't well supported by evidence. Back in 2007 a review was done of seven studies that investigated the effects of stretching after exercise (Herber & Noronha, 2007). They found that these studies consistently showed there was minimal or no effect on the muscle soreness experienced between half a day and three days after the physical activity.

So a cool-down won't necessarily stop you aching, and studies have also shown that it may not even help significantly when it comes to avoiding injury (although more research needs to be done on that). But of course, there are other valid reasons for doing a cool-down, namely being able to safely ease your body down from intense levels, and also to allow stretching to take place.

Why should you stretch after exercise?
Stretching helps develop flexibility and keeps muscles at their optimal length, meaning they're less likely to be imbalanced and cause you problems. A tight hamstring, for example, can be a contributing factor in some instances of back pain.

Chances are you don't get many opportunities to stretch. If you have a desk-job, or spend lots of time in fairly static positions, your body could do with a good stretch every once in a while. It will help loosen all the imbalances and muscle tightening that might be occurring from spending eight hours a day hunched over a computer.

Stretching is best done when your muscles are warm and supple. If 5-a-side is one of your only forms of exercise then the period straight after the game represents a golden opportunity to get this valuable stretching done.

If you have a desk-job, your body could do with a good stretch

Static stretching tips

Done wrong, stretching can be dangerous so make sure that you:

Stretch when you are warm. Do it directly after the game, not 15 minutes later after you've driven home

Stretch only to the point of slight discomfort. If you go past this point you're at risk of causing yourself an injury. If you do feel pain, stop immediately

Don't round your back as you stretch – the stress this can place on your lower back can cause problems

Breathe as you stretch, don't hold your breath

A simple cool-down routine won't win you any prizes for looking good, nor will it help you be first to the bar afterwards, but it makes a lot of sense

Sleep Like a Champion

It is the night before your weekly 5-a-side game. You're desperate to end a five-game losing streak. Start by turning off late-night poker and getting some kip. The benefits will be huge

The great George Weah, former Ballon d'Or winner and now Senator for Montserrado County in Liberia, was once asked for the secret of his success. 'I sleep for 12 hours every night,' he said. Roger Federer? 12 hours. LeBron James? 12 hours. See a pattern? No? Then it's past your bedtime.

George, Roger and LeBron know a bit about athletic performance, and we should all listen very closely to them. Sleep is not just essential to our overall well-being, it has a direct and significant relation to how we play 5-a-side football.

Here comes the sciencey bit
A study published by the American Academy of Pediatrics showed that adolescent athletes who slept eight or more hours each night were 68 percent less likely to be injured than athletes who regularly slept less.

Lack of sleep can affect cognitive skills and fine motor skills, meaning that you can be off your game for no reason other than just not having enough sleep. Work done by Cheri Mah – summarised in the amazing infographic on page 86 – shows some quite astonishing results of getting enough sleep:

Tennis players get a 42% boost in hitting accuracy during depth drills.

Sleep extension provides swimmers a 17% improvement in reaction time off the starting block.

Sleep improves split-second decision making ability by 4.3%

American Football players drop 0.1s off their 40-yard dash times by sleeping more.

It's not too much of a stretch to believe that these findings on accuracy, reaction times and decision-making could all reasonably translate across to forms of football. Just imagine how much a 42% increase in accuracy could improve your 5-a-side.

If you're the sort of person who prefers the metaphorical stick rather than the carrot, it's also worth understanding that insufficient sleep can lead to all sorts of negative effects:

Chronic sleep loss can lead to a 30-40% reduction in glucose metabolism

Sleep loss can mean an 11% reduction in the time to exhaustion

Maximum bench press drops 20lbs after 4 days of restricted sleep

So it's pretty conclusive that sleep directly impacts your performance on the field – no wonder that most top athletes already recognise this.

In his book *The Gold Mine Effect,* Rasums Ankerson spent time with both the world renowned Kenyan and Ethiopian distance runners. He found that in their training regimes they value rest and recovery in a way that few people do in the West.

As triple steeplechase world champion Moses Kiptanui told Ankerson: 'Recovery is as important as training. But not recovery in the sense most people understand it. If your brain is working while you are recovering, it means that you're actually not recovering at all.'

As former half-marathon world champion Lornah Kiplagat says: 'During the periods when I train hardest, I spend 16 hours a day in bed.'

Better living through sleep

For us non-elite athletes, the challenge is to get a sufficient amount of sleep to allow you to function at your full capacity in your job, social life, family and of course your weekly game of 5-a-side.

Sleep boosts our brain cell numbers, protecting our brain circuitry. Conversely, lost sleep leads to a loss of brain cells and, worse still, being deprived of sleep has been linked to stress responses and disruptions in gene function that could affect metabolism, inflammation, and long-term disease risk.

In fact, the effects of not getting enough sleep can arguably multiply beyond the direct effects caused by not being able to perform sufficient repair processes to brain and body overnight.

Sleep deprivation has been identified as a major contributing factor to sapping willpower, which means that staying away from potential vices such as cigarettes, alcohol, or the wrong types of food is going to be a lot harder, and your ability to find the willpower to make positive changes, such as sticking to fitness goals, is also at risk. Breaking it down into terms we are more comfortable with, you are less likely to sacrifice yourself by tracking that runner you kind of know is about to score against your team if you are sleep deprived. First, you won't have the energy. Second, you won't have the will. You will have become a baggy-eyed loser.

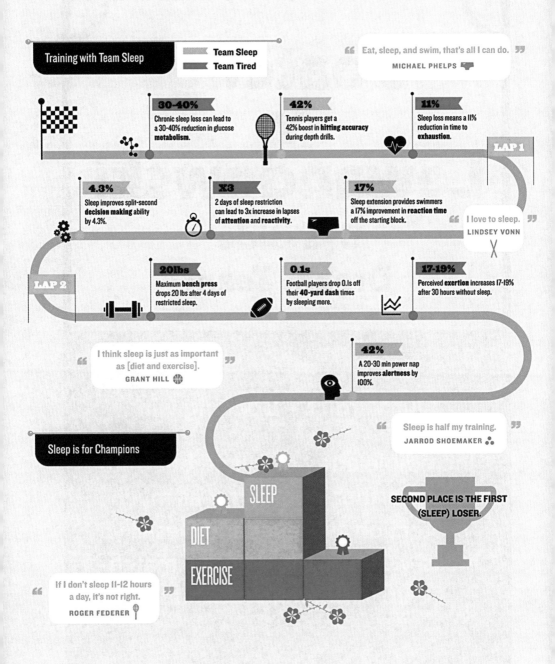

Training with Team Sleep

Team Sleep
Team Tired

" Eat, sleep, and swim, that's all I can do. "
MICHAEL PHELPS

30-40%
Chronic sleep loss can lead to a 30-40% reduction in glucose **metabolism**.

42%
Tennis players get a 42% boost in **hitting accuracy** during depth drills.

11%
Sleep loss means a 11% reduction in time to **exhaustion**.

LAP 1

4.3%
Sleep improves split-second **decision making** ability by 4.3%.

X3
2 days of sleep restriction can lead to 3x increase in lapses of **attention** and **reactivity**.

17%
Sleep extension provides swimmers a 17% improvement in **reaction time** off the starting block.

" I love to sleep. "
LINDSEY VONN

LAP 2

20lbs
Maximum **bench press** drops 20 lbs after 4 days of restricted sleep.

0.1s
Football players drop 0.1s off their **40-yard dash** times by sleeping more.

17-19%
Perceived **exertion** increases 17-19% after 30 hours without sleep.

" I think sleep is just as important as [diet and exercise]. "
GRANT HILL

42%
A 20-30 min power nap improves **alertness** by 100%.

" Sleep is half my training. "
JARROD SHOEMAKER

Sleep is for Champions

SLEEP
DIET
EXERCISE

SECOND PLACE IS THE FIRST (SLEEP) LOSER.

" If I don't sleep 11-12 hours a day, it's not right. "
ROGER FEDERER

Boateng
v
Lewandowski
5-a-side
Dream Team

Our Verdict – Boateng win

Incredible array of talent, but Cafu and Barthez don't offer as much protection as Neuer and Desailly. Messi v Cafu is the decisive match-up in Boateng's favour

Manuel Neuer

Marcel Desailly

Patrick Vieira

Andrés Iniesta

Leo Messi

Thierry Henry

Zinedine Zidane

Cafu

Fabio Cannavaro

Fabian Barthez

How To Play Until You're 70

If you love 5-a-side then you'll want to play for as long as humanly possible. We spoke to George Greig, who is still dominating his weekly game as he enters his eighth decade

You'll be playing a game one day and ask yourself the dreaded question, the ultimate foundation-shaker: "Am I too old to be playing 5-a-side?"

To make it simple for you, we've devised a little test that you can do to determine if you should still be playing 5-a-side.

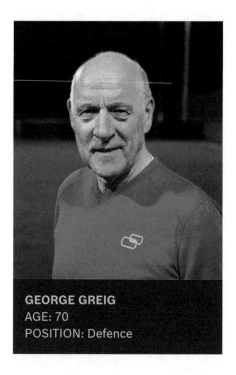

GEORGE GREIG
AGE: 70
POSITION: Defence

Answer this simple question:
Are you still breathing? If you answered 'yes' then congratulations! You can continue playing 5-a-side. There are so many physical and mental benefits that it is more damaging to stop. George Greig, 70, outruns men half his age on the 5-a-side pitch every week. Is he superhuman? A freak of nature? No, as George tells us, it is more about a mental attitude than it is about physical gifts...

George: I have played 5-a-side every Tuesday night for the last 33 years. In the winter months we play indoors and in the summer we move outdoors. The questions I assume that would jump to people's mind are:

1. Is he any good, or is he just tip-toeing around and the others going easy on him?

2. What is the standard like?

The first one is hard for me to answer, but I reckon I am reasonably competitive and nobody treats me like a delicate flower. The standard? Probably half the guys have played amateur 11-a-side and the others are enthusiastic players better suited to 5-a-side. The average age is about 42, including me in the calculation. I played 11-a-side for a couple of good amateur teams for about 18 years and packed it in at 36 – not because I couldn't do it anymore. The team just ran out of decent players and rather than get humped regularly, we stopped entering the league. The team had a two-hour indoor training night, which

George's Fives Survival Tips

no.1

Figure out which is their bad foot and always show them on to it. It nearly always works – how many genuinely two–footed players do you know?

no.2

Always get tight on to the guys with the crap first touch

no.3

Even if you can't get a tackle in, put pressure on them – it is usually enough to put them off and lead to a wayward shot or mishit pass

no.4

Finally, for the really quick guys, there is always obstruction!

we kept going. This is the first key thing that helped me play for so long – we still have that same night, 33 years on and have never stopped training and playing. Never stop – it is a big factor.

A lot of things accumulate to being fit at 70 but it has nothing to do with being any different from any other naturally fit people. People say your age is in your head – well, so is your fitness. My pet hate: The guy that says: "Thought you were right on it tonight," and just when you are allowing yourself a little inner smile he adds "for a guy of 70". If you've had a good game, you've had a good game.

I have been lucky with injuries. Good genes have played a part, but I always warm-up properly. About seven years ago, I had a big problem with muscle wastage in my knees, which was preventing me twisting and turning as normal. A personal trainer gave me a set of exercises aimed at building up my leg muscles and promoting blood flow. They worked and I still do them to this day.

You do slow down as you get older, but nothing like as much as you might think. We always trained hard. Short, sharp sprints, which were done competitively, really helped. It's given me a solid base. Anyway, 5-a-side pitches are pretty small and if you know where to be, speed is almost irrelevant.

My fitness is miles better at 70 than it was at 60. I am surprised myself.

Until five years ago, all I did was a lot of swimming and 5-a-side. Since I retired, I go to the gym twice a week and a Body Balance class. My gym routine is a 2.5k run with a pretty gentle start to warm up. Then two sets of 15 knee lifts of 40kg; then a set of 15 x 20 kg on each knee individually. Some stretching exercises for hamstring, rotation, and a little abdominal stuff. Then another 2.5k run – this time a bit faster – and then repeat all the previous exercises. Shower and back home. Body Balance is a mix of core strength, balance exercise and yoga flexibility. It's an intense 50-minute session – the best workout I have ever done.

When I finished playing 11-a-side, I really struggled mentally. It had been a huge part of my life for such a long time and I really missed it. There is nothing like banging in a goal and winning a couple of 50/50 tackles to put you at peace with the world. So, for me, 5-a-side has never been just about the fitness. It is great socially, too. We still keep in touch with former players and have the occasional night out.

It's not about living like a monk. It's about a balanced lifestyle. I chucked smoking at 22 because it was affecting my football. I have never been a big drinker but I have a glass of wine most nights and eat lots of pasta and rice. Having said that, I still have a fairly regular curry. Again, it's about balance. I used to think buying another pair of trainers was an act of faith – not any more.

Food and Drink

Nutrition is a massive part of sporting performance. With just a few adjustments to what you put into your body before and after a game, you could see major benefits

Part One
Food

What to Eat Before Football

Turning up to a game of football without a proper pre-match meal is like lining up on the starting grid of a race without any fuel in your car. You don't stand a chance of achieving your potential if you have not found the pre-game combination that works for you. And that's the key here. There is no magic formula, but learning the framework will help you find the right fuel for your gleaming, turbo-charged engine.

Fuel for your engine

Pre-match, your focus has to be on carbohydrates. The right kind, and the right amount.

Carbohydrate is converted to glycogen, which in turn powers your muscle movement.

The good news: your body can store glycogen – both in the muscles and in the liver.

The bad news: it can only store limited amounts and that store is always depleting. Your glycogen stores need to be topped up regularly because they deplete as you expend energy, and even as you sleep!

Before exercise you want to make sure that your store of glycogen is at capacity. If not, you're going to feel weak and unable to hit your top gear, something that most of us have experienced at some point in the past.

But you don't want to put any old fuel into that F1 engine you're packing. Some foods are better for your body's glycogen stores than others. When it comes to pre-match meals, starchy carbohydrates are your friend as they are best at breaking down into glycogen.

Starchy carbs include potatoes, breads, cereal, pasta, fruits and vegetables. These foods are digested at a rate that provides consistent energy to the body and are emptied from the stomach in two to three hours (though they will stay in your intestine and colon for longer, and that's fine).

How much to eat before a game

If you really want to be at your best, eat carbohydrate-rich foods in quantities somewhere between **1-4 g of carbs per kg of body weight** before competing, where your game is over 60 minutes.

Given that most games of 5-a-side are less than an hour (and to avoid over-eating, since that's just going to make you put on weight), try starting off at 1g/kg of carbs and work up from there if it's not enough.

For most people, 1g/kg is going to be absolutely fine for a 40-minute game of football.

An average sized man, about 70kg, should eat a pre-match meal of around 70g of carbs. Examples of these kinds of meals are coming up.

When to eat before a game

Advice varies on when to eat. It boils down to two things: (i) your personal preference and (ii) what you're eating (smoothies, for example, are quickly digested). Despite there being some variation, pretty much all of the experts agree that you should eat between one and four hours before you play.

We recommend eating **two to three hours before you play** to ensure your meal is digested properly. If you're in any doubt, it makes sense to eat earlier rather than later. If you feel hungry before the game, you can always top up with a snack, but if you eat your meal too late then you could end up feeling bloated and heavy for the game, as well as not giving your body enough time to break the meal down into the energy it needs.

It's not carbo-loading!

A lot of people have an idea that before sport you need to 'carbo load', and in their heads this often involves consuming obscene quantities of pasta eaten out of bowls the size of buckets. This is **not** what it's about.

Your daily carb intake will usually be between 7-12g per kg of body weight, so you can see that the 1-4g per kg of body weight in your pre-game meal isn't an insane attempt at eating incredible amounts of carbs, it's really just a normal-sized healthy meal of high-quality carbs.

1. Jacket potato with tuna & sweetcorn

2. Pasta with sauce

3. Sports drink and energy bar

4. Sandwich and a banana

5. Sandwich, banana, nuts and fruit juice

6. Weetabix with banana

75g
of carbs

01

81g
of carbs

02

Eat two to three hours before you play to ensure your meal is digested properly – if you eat your meal too late then you could end up feeling bloated

Four common pre-match meal mistakes

At some point most of us have got it wrong, sometimes resulting in pretty unpleasant consequences. When people do go wrong it's very often as a result of timing (which all stems from a lack of preparation):

Eating too early – you give your body a good top-up of fuel, but your reserves have depleted too much by game-time. That big lunch will not see you through for a 7pm kick-off. It'll just leave you feeling like a shell of a man as you run out of steam in the last 20 minutes. That runner that scored the three late goals that cost your team the win? That was your guy.

Eating too late – it takes time for the body to digest a meal and turn carbohydrates into glycogen. Panic eating too close to the game will result in you carrying around all the weight of the food but without its energy. Your body hasn't had time to process it.

If it isn't the timing, it's **what** people eat. Stick to starchy carbs and avoid either of these rookie errors:

Eating too much protein or fat – protein foods take longer to digest than starch, so eat moderate protein meals. Fats take even longer still, meaning that you might not feel settled by game time. A fry-up might sound like a great plan before football, but you'll have just as much chance of digesting your own football boots in time for the game.

Eating too much sugar – sugar can give you energy quickly, but it can sometimes cause rapid energy swings, and the end result can actually be that you have less energy during the game. You might use some high-sugar foods before a game, but make sure a good portion of your pre-game meal is high-nutrient starchy carbohydrates.

Part Two
Drink

What should I drink before football?

In preparing your pre-game meal, don't overlook the importance of keeping yourself hydrated. Dehydration of more than 2% of your bodyweight can have a dramatic negative impact on performance.

Hydrating properly *isn't* just a case of trying to drink as much as possible before the game. In fact that can be a dangerous thing to do.

Sports drink manufacturer Powerade suggest **slowly consuming 5–7 ml of fluid (not necessarily a sports drink) per kilogram of body weight starting 4 hours before the game.** That's between 350 and 500ml for a 70kg individual.

About two hours before exercise they recommend that if you haven't produced urine, or the urine is dark (a sign of mild dehydration), then more fluid should be consumed (e.g. 3–5 ml/kg of body weight).

Sports drinks vs water

You don't need to look very hard to see big-money pro footballers necking a bottle of the latest sports drink – usually provided to them free of charge by the sponsors. The debate around the benefits of these drinks has been raging for years, and it's complicated.

Lucozade sponsor the FA Premier League in England, Powerade was an official sponsor of the 2014 Brazil World Cup, and Gatorade sponsor a host of mainly non-football events. Sports drinks are a multi-billion dollar industry and the makers of these drinks sell the idea that their product can unlock our inner Messi. Don't buy into all the hype without looking behind the advertising and understanding what sports drinks are all about.

What's the secret formula?

Sports drinks are a combination of plain old water plus three things: sodium, carbohydrate and flavourings.

Carbohydrate is simply sugar, and is necessary in order to provide fuel for working muscles. It replaces your glycogen energy stores.

Sodium is salt, and a small amount of this helps speed up re-hydration. It maintains your fluid balance and replaces the salts that are lost in sweating.

Flavourings are what make the whole thing taste nice, unless you enjoy drinking water mixed with nothing but sugar and salt.

In summary: water, plus sugar, plus salt, plus something to make it taste nice.

Although all sports drinks are some concoction of carbohydrate and sodium, the different brands combine them in slightly (or sometimes significantly) different quantities and it's worth understanding the results.

Isotonic, Hypotonic, and Hypertonic
You have heard the term **isotonic,** right? Any idea what it means?

If a sport drinks is isotonic it means that it contains similar concentrations of salt and sugar as in the human body. That seems like a sensible idea; you want to be drinking something that replaces fluid and gives you the same proportions of sugar and salt that are in line with your body's natural balance.

There's only so much sodium that you can add to a drink (and too much can be dangerous), so the noticeable difference between the different brands tends to be the level of sugar that's added.

The level of sugar is the main driver behind drinks being labelled **hypotonic** (which means that it contain a lower concentration of salt and sugar than the human body) or **hypertonic** (containing a higher concentration of salt and sugar than the human body).

When you look at the difference in carbs (sugar) between each type of drink you might find this quite startling and maybe a little overwhelming – which of these is best to drink for football?

FLAVOURED WATER
(all that most people need to drink for exercise)

450ml water

50ml squash
(reduced sugar)

Most people don't need to consume a sports drink for the activity that they do

If you're not doing any exercise at all then drinking a sports drink is just adding extra calories. Even if you are doing exercise, research indicates that if you're doing shorter sessions, less than about 60 minutes, then you really shouldn't need anything other than water.

Worst of all, if you're trying to lose weight then a sports drink could be counteracting the calories you're burning playing football. If weight-loss is your goal and you do want to drink a sports drink then try to stick to the hypotonic drinks, which contain less sugar.

Drinking a sports drink can be beneficial

If you're performing intense exercise that is going on for longer than 60-90 minutes, your muscles should benefit from the top-up of glycogen it gets from the sugars in a sports drink. The Journal of Applied Physiology found that consuming an isotonic sports drink increased treadmill running time to exhaustion by 27% in recreational runners (but bear in mind that a lot of these types of studies have been found to be flawed for the amateur athlete in one way or another).

Secondly, if you're going into a game without having eaten for a long while beforehand – say immediately after work – then an isotonic sports drink can give you a top-up of carbohydrate which could cover your energy deficit, although it's still preferable to try to have eaten properly instead.

Hypertonic drinks, which contain more than 10% of sugar (e.g. a cola drink) are never suitable to be drunk during a game. Not only do they generally contain gas that makes them harder to drink, the high sugar content actually means they have a low gastric emptying rate, or in other words the body isn't that effective at turning all that sugar into energy.

But even hypertonic drinks might have a use under the right circumstances. After a very long session you might consider drinking one of these high sugar drinks to help replace your depleted energy reserves, especially in the first 60 minutes or so after exercise in order to speed your recovery the most. It's not a great substitute for having a proper meal and drinking water but sometimes the situation doesn't allow for it, so a sugary drink can be a viable second best.

The most important thing is that you drink something

Drinking a sports drink can't always give you an edge, but failure to drink enough fluid is guaranteed to impair your performance. Studies have shown that dehydration of just 2% of your body weight can have a large negative impact on performance. Make sure you drink enough before, during and after football to ensure that you're hydrated going into the game and then replace any fluid lost through sweating.

So even though a sports drink probably isn't going to improve your performance in your one-hour game of 5-a-side, if it means that you drink enough fluid before, during and after sport then having one might not be such a bad thing. Some of us prefer the convenience and taste of a sports drink over and above the alternatives and, if you're happy paying the extra instead of filling a bottle with cheap squash and water, then don't let anyone stop you drinking them.

REAL FRUIT SPORTS DRINK

Pinch of salt

250ml water

250ml fruit juice
(100% pure juice)

No single plan fits everyone
– test, test and test again

We're all different shapes and sizes and respond differently to what we eat and drink. What works for one person might not work for another. The only real way to find the perfect meal for you is to start off with the guidelines above and then adjust it for your needs. Experiment with different foods and timing of your meal until you get the right combination.

Each time you try something new, listen to your body and use it as feedback.

Did you feel weak and lethargic or fully fuelled and in peak condition? Experiment, test and refine until you find your perfect set-up.

Experiment with different foods and timing of your meal until you get the right combination

EASY HOME MADE SPORTS DRINK

4tsp sugar (optional)

Pinch of salt

400ml water

100 ml squash (not sugar-free variety)

5-a-side

MOJITO-INSPIRED SPORTS DRINK

4-6 mint leaves

330ml water

Juice of ½ a lime (20 ml)

Pinch of salt

150ml apple juice

1 tsp brown sugar

MANUFACTURED SPORTS DRINKS

Key ingredients (based on 500ml)

30-35g carbs (sugars)

Small amounts of sodium (salt)

Flavourings

Part Three
Refuel

Post-match refuel
Recovery and Repair

A good game of 5-a-side will put your body through its paces, depleting your energy stores and leaving your muscles in need of repair. In order to aid your recovery and get your body back on track, you need to consider when and how you refuel it after a game. If you don't, your recovery will be delayed, meaning that your body is going to feel the effects for longer.

What do I need after a game?

If you've played a hard game, your body is going to be crying out for three things: carbohydrates, protein and fluid.

Carbohydrates: these replace your glycogen (energy) stores that will have been used during the game. They can be replaced with simple carbohydrates (sugary carbs, like sports drinks, sweets and fruit) as these are quickly absorbed by the body. You should take on at least 50g of carbohydrate in the 1-2 hours post exercise, beginning as soon as possible.

Protein: This is essential to repair your muscles. FIFA's nutritional guidelines suggest that an intake of small amounts, approximately 20-25g of high quality protein, enhances your body's growth and repair during the recovery period.

Fluid: your body will have lost fluid through sweat so it is important that you top-up after exercise. For every kg of weight lost in a game, you would need to drink between 1.2-1.5 litres of fluid as replacement. However, it's unlikely that you'll lose that much in a game of 5-a-side, so just drink what feels comfortable – when your urine runs clear, you're hydrated again.

When should I begin refuelling?

Refuelling is most important over the first 1-2 hours after exercise but ideally you should begin taking food and liquid as soon as possible after any strenuous exercise. The sooner you get fuel inside you, the sooner your body can repair and return to its normal state.

Refuelling options

The top choice: a full, balanced meal post game.

For instance, an omelette (3 large eggs, cheese) will contain over 20g of protein, and if you ate that with two slices of brown bread and a glass of fruit juice you'd be well over 50g of carbs – a perfect refuelling combination.

In fact, if you picture nearly any healthy meal that involves some meat, fish, or eggs plus some high quality carbohydrates, a normal serving size should be adequate to refuel you properly, especially if you have been playing 5-a-side for less than 1 hour.

SOURCES OF 10g PROTEIN:

Animal Protein (high quality)	Vegetable Protein
2 small eggs	4 slices bread
300ml cow's milk	90g breakfast cereal
30g cheese	2 cups cooked pasta
200g yoghurt	3 cups rice
35-50g meat, fish or chicken	60g nuts / seeds

Source: FIFA Nutrition for football

If you have a drive home, take your recovery food and drink with you to consume straight after the game

On the other hand, if you aren't able to put together a proper meal, then you could try food supplements: such as an instant shake. You can buy mixes that are both high in protein and carbohydrate, though you'll have to do a bit of careful searching for these as most protein powders contain a minimal amount of carbs.

You'll find powders that are high in protein and carbs often labelled as 'gainers' or as giving you 'mass'. A search on any good bodybuilding store and a good read of the nutritional information should give you what you need.

Equally, you can get sports bars that do the trick – again, read the label to get what you need.

The great thing about these bars is that they are really convenient, even if they're not quite as satisfying as real food. Beware though, people use these to gain weight and, if you haven't burned off enough calories to support the intake from your shake then that's exactly what will happen to you – and don't assume that this weight will be muscle!

As with all nutrition, the art of getting it right is by experimenting. Our bodies are all different and so is the intensity and type of football we play. Your needs after 40 minutes of 5-a-side will be different to 90 minutes of 11-a-side.

The evening game

For recreational 5-a-side players, games often take place in the evening, sometimes with late kick-offs. In these circumstances it can be hard to refuel before sleep – once you are home it can be a bit late to cook, or even to eat a full meal.

The key to avoiding problems here is preparation. If you have a drive home then take your recovery food and drink with you to consume straight after the game, letting it settle on your way home. You need to strike a balance between satisfying the need for refuelling, and eating so late that it disturbs your sleep.

One simple, but effective solution is to take a bottle of chocolate milk with you (in addition to water to replace fluids). The chocolate milk contains sugar, which helps restore energy, and also naturally-occurring proteins, which help with the muscle repair process. It's a well known recovery source and it tastes good too – there's a whole US-based website dedicated to it as a sports recovery drink: gotchocolatemilk.org

If you just threw this 330ml bottle of chocolate milk into your sports bag with a banana then you've got an instant refuel kit you can consume very quickly in the car home from the game.

Tales from the pitch

Champion Hurdler

By Jack Carr

About 10 years ago I played in a team of mates in a local league. When we were in the mood we could be a match for anyone, although inconsistencies, blunders and a squad rotation policy usually meant we coasted in as mid-table also-rans.

The better teams went hard on us because we often played well against them, and the rubbish teams also targeted us because they thought they'd be able to beat us if we had one of our all-too-common off days.

Amid the drudgery of another mid-table campaign, something magical happened. We were locked in a tense game against fellow mid-table battlers – a group of hardened 30-somethings (we were lads in our early 20s).

There had already been a bit of 'handbags', enough to have everyone on edge. I can't remember anything about the goal that broke the deadlock, but it was our team who scored with only a couple of minutes to spare. We erupted in celebration.

The other team were heads down, swearing at everything – each other, the ref, us. One of their defenders, an old-hand, bent down to tie his laces.

As we continued to draw-out our celebration a bit longer than we should have, our euphoric goalscorer, seeing the shoelace-tier crouched on the floor, ran up behind him at some pace and leapt over him. It felt like he got about 30 seconds of hang-time on that jump as the rest of us looked on in horror, praying that the guy wouldn't stand up midway through being hurdled and leave them both pole-axed.

Our euphoric goalscorer, seeing the shoelace-tier crouched on the floor, ran up behind him at some pace and leapt over him

Fortunately, my team-mate cleared him in what really was a magnificent display of hurdling. As it turned out, there is nothing that will wind-up an opponent more than the feeling that they've just been involuntarily hurdled. After finishing tying his laces and computing what had just occurred, the human-hurdle flew into an incredible rage. The referee, as well as four or five players, had to step in to diffuse the situation as the hurdler finished his celebrations, only then realising how daft he'd been.

Somehow, we got the game restarted, and hung on for a win. Most importantly, we made it out of there with our legs unbroken.

There are lots of things I can't remember about that night – but what will live with me forever is the image of my friend, smile on his face, leaping over the angriest man in the world.

Peter Krustrup

The 5-a-side Professor

How do you get fitter, happier and make lots of friends? One Danish academic has discovered that when it comes to mental and physical well-being, nothing beats fives

In 2003, Professor Peter Krustrup, from the University of Copenhagen in Denmark, began to look at the mental and physical health benefits of football. Today, over 70 research papers have been published on the subject, with a huge body of evidence pointing to the benefits of 5-a-side football in particular. We caught up with the '5-a-side Professor'...

01

How did you first get involved in researching the benefits of football?
I was a researcher studying match performance, fatigue and the effects of training among elite footballers. I started using the same technology on recreational and veteran footballers. We saw that the heart rate during 5-a-side was as high as for elite players.
So we did a pilot project which involved a 12-week training period. We actually looked for the poorest teams in Denmark and investigated their training, matches and also the effects of the 12-week football programme. Even though the players we studied weren't good, they showed very high intensity levels. At the same time it was also fun and social – we found out that if football could benefit them, then it could benefit everybody.

And you found many specific health benefits such as blood pressure, fat loss...

Some of the very impressive results relate to heart function and aerobic fitness, which increased by as much as 15% within just three months. The effect on blood pressure is important too. In many studies, there are decreases in blood pressure of 10mm of mercury after just three months of training, which is as much as a very effective treatment with pills. However, a pill gives a lowering of blood pressure but no other positive effects, whereas football provides other positive effects at the same time – lower cholesterol, lower resting heart rate and lower body fat.

We have also observed that bone mineralisation is increased by as much as 2-3% in mature women within three months. In one study we looked into the lowering of the risk of cardiovascular disease – it was lowered by 50% in a group of homeless men, and also groups of hypertensive men and women. In another study we looked at the heart function of diabetic men and observed that their hearts – in terms of one of the key variables relating to elasticity – became 10 years younger after just three months of training.

The research seems to also suggest that football is a better form of exercise than swimming and cycling, and as good as running...

There are now more than 70 research articles across 20 different journals. In many of these research papers we compare the effects of small-sided football with other types of training. The conclusions are that football is a very intense, versatile and effective all-in-one type of training, which combines endurance, high intensity and strength training. From football, we see the same benefits as strength training in terms of musculoskeletal health; the same benefits on metabolic health as endurance training; and the same cardiovascular effects with football as high-intensity interval training. Football is the only type of training that combines all three.

In terms of the health impacts, is 5-a-side better than 11-a-side?

The pilot studies have investigated both 5-a-side football, 7-a-side and 11-a-side. The exercise intensity is similar, involving the same heart rate and many specific intense actions like sprints, turns and dribbles, shots, jumps. But the so-called 'Football Fitness' concept we have developed is based on small-sided football, like 5-a-side, on small pitches with few players so that intensity is high. Involvement is also key – so plenty of ball touches and many technical actions for all the players, which you may not see in an 11-a-side situation.

5-a-side...

- Is a safer and more effective form of exercise than 11-a-side football

- Is better all-in-one training for you than most other forms of exercise – including cycling, swimming, walking

- Reduces blood pressure and resting heart rate

- Reduces body fat

- Lowers cholesterol levels

- Improves heart function and aerobic fitness

- Strengthens your muscles and bones, and improves postural balance

- Works your body harder than other forms of exercise – but makes you feel like you are working less than other activities

- Decreases worry levels in men

- Boosts self-confidence

In 5-a-side football, there are also much less injuries than during 11-a-side games. Many studies have shown that the number of injuries in small-sided training is just 20% of the number of injuries in competitive 11-a-side games.

I believe that the enjoyment factor of 5-a-side football is a key part of why it is so good for you...

Although the intensity levels are very high, players report that the perceived exertion is moderate. Whereas high-intensity exercises are generally considered very hard, on a scale of 0-10, the men reported a '3.9' and the women a '5.5'. In the same study, a group of men and women runners both reported an '8.0'. As a football player you are focusing on your team-mates and opponents and the game itself, rather than the physical strain.

And there are big psychological benefits too...

Our sports psychologists have used various types of questionnaires related to wellbeing, the feeling of flow during training and matches, and also worry levels. They found out that you don't worry during football – you think about the game, the team-mates and your role. You forget about everyday life when you are on the pitch. We have also seen in many studies that people get a more positive body image, gain more self-confidence and gain a more positive attitude towards team sports. When you ask players about football, they always talk about 'we' stories – common experiences for the team. That [togetherness] makes it much easier for people to get to know each other, which helps adherence to physical activity.

01   Professor Peter Krustrup

02   The Prof shows his skills

03   Togetherness makes it much easier for people to get to know each other

Tales from the pitch

Brolly to the Throttle

By Stewart Holland

We were playing in a 5-a-side tournament in Perth, Scotland. A couple of guys were local but most lived about 30 miles away. Anyway, we had a company car so we drove there.

The tournament was going well; we played some good football and made the quarter-finals. We were losing and just before the end of the game I took a shot. Just as I did, their big defender caught me right on the ankle. Instant pain.

My immediate thought was that the ligaments had gone.

The tournament finished and we went to the pub for some liquid refreshment.

The pain was so bad that I couldn't bear even to drink a pint. It didn't stop my team-mates, though. The beers were flowing and, after a few rounds, out of nowhere came the question:

"Who's driving home?"

All eyes descended on me. At this point, I was sitting on a chair with my foot up and a towel of ice on my ankle. I couldn't even walk so had no chance of driving home as I wouldn't be able to use the accelerator.

Now, as this was a company car, it was packed with essentials: jackets, umbrellas etc. Then, someone came up with the idea that I could use an umbrella for the throttle. Now, try and imagine changing gear whilst pushing / pulling a brolly on / off the accelerator... you've never heard a car scream so much as that night. Fortunately, most of the journey was dual carriageway but it was still a precarious task.

The next day the hospital confirmed that I had torn my ankle ligaments. The things you do for a game of 5-a-side.

Legends of 5-a-side

The Cat

Excellence in goalkeeping has garnered the same nickname since the first excellent goalkeepers kept goal excellently. The Cat. It's about agility, the ability to spring into action instantly. Roger Paul Noveal is the biggest Cat in the fives jungle

If you are very good, your team-mates might start calling you The Cat. If you are very, very good, perhaps your rep will spread to the rest of your league, and you will be known as The Cat, even though there may be others. The Cat of Cats. *Gatto di tutti Gatto.*

So how good do you have to be before everybody everywhere they play 5-a-side calls you The Cat?

Meet Roger Paul Noveal **(below left)**. You can call him The Cat.

01

Does everyone call you that?
People sometimes call me Roger and quite a few call me my middle name Paul, but nowadays on the 5-a-side circuit they all just call me The Cat.

How did you get started in goal?
When I was young I played on the right wing for a London team called River Hawks, which was a competitor to Senrab, the famous youth team that produced the likes of Sol Campbell, John Terry and dozens of other pros (although a little after my time). It was a footballing hotbed.

One day one of the boys told the teacher at school that I could play in goal. If you don't want to play in goal, don't play well when you get put there. The problem was that I did, so they kept me there and I tried to make the position my own.

After I left school I played semi-pro for Eastbourne Borough, and things were good. I was playing in the early rounds of the FA Cup, the FA Vase and enjoying it, but not taking it particularly seriously considering it was at quite a good level of football. In the end the travelling from London down to the south coast made it a bit difficult and I gave it up because I was getting more money from my job working for the London Electricity Board.

I played for a lot of London teams, but the pre-season training was a killer!

When did you come to 5-a-side?

When I was a kid I played in a 5-a-side tournament with my brother and I found it enjoyable, but 5-a-side wasn't really big then. I didn't start playing 5-a-side again until 2002, when I started to see that a few of the tournaments had some good prizes. I played 11-a-side for years and all I got was trophies and medals, but the 5-a-side tournaments were giving out holidays, money, prizes!

I wasn't really good enough, but I won a tournament on a penalty shoot-out and suddenly I thought my team were really good. The next year I went to the same tournament and we didn't even make it out of the group stages, which was a big come-down. I realised we needed to be better, so I started putting together another team from the players in my 11-a-side team.

You ran into the legendary Sof pretty early on, didn't you?

I had started hearing about a player who was supposed to be a bit special, but hadn't yet seen him. Then in 2003 I was playing in a tournament and my team was knocked out in the quarter-finals. I stuck around to watch the other games and I saw this guy and looked at his first touch; his movement on the ball, it was sublime. Just watching him nonchalantly caressing the ball; I always thought that the Brazilians had the ball stuck to their feet, but this guy was something else.

After the game I said 'Where have you played, I know you've played somewhere'. He just looked at me, smiled and said 'You good keeper, I see you'. The guy just made me laugh but the next thing I knew his team, Black Cats, had invited me to play for them the following day in a tournament in Manchester.

I didn't have a car, but that wasn't going to stop me. On the morning of the tournament I picked up a hire car then went to pick up Sof and the rest of the guys. My dad drove us and we ended up going the wrong way, making us late for the tournament. They'd saved our games so we had to play them all back-to-back when we arrived, but still we beat absolutely everybody and won the tournament. We had some exceptional players. The prize for winning the tournament was a holiday to Ibiza. It was surreal – I'd only met this team yesterday and here I was going off on holiday with

I used to play 11-a-side, but the 5-a-side tournaments were giving out better prizes!

them! Sof and I became great friends from that point.

Sof is the best 5-a-side player ever, without a shadow of a doubt. Nowadays when you see people with their flip-flap skill, he brought that to the game. He would play against semi-professional teams and absolutely ruin them. They'd ask who he played for, but he just told them he played 5-a-side. The other players who are good have elements of his game, but he was the original, the master.

What's the weirdest situation you've found yourself in at a tournament?
I later formed a team called Liberties, which Sof joined me in. We won a lot of tournaments, around 10-12 nationals since starting in 2006.

We once had two tournaments that we qualified for on the same day. One was run by Xbox and had a £5000 prize, the other was run by Powerade and offered a trip to the Euros with £1000 cash. We could only do one of the tournaments so we called up another team that hadn't qualified and we did a deal that they would play in the Powerade tournament as long as we got the £1000 if they won. Lo and behold they won theirs, and we ended up losing ours!

Why do you love 5-a-side?

The great thing about 5-a-side is that as a goalkeeper I get to do a lot of work. It suits me because I'm a good shot stopper.

The main difference between 11-a-side and 5-a-side is that you're involved so much more. If you're playing a 20-minute game, you're involved much more than in a 90-minute 11-a-side game, which means you can have much more of an impact on the result.

In 90 minutes of 11-a-side, you might only get four or five shots on target. I reckon I get about 40 shots at my goal in a 50-minute game of 5-a-side. Everybody can score from anywhere and when teams realise that you start to see the potential of the 5-a-side game.

I reckon I get about 40 shots at my goal in a 50-minute game of 5-a-side

05

06

01 The Cat (left) and fellow 5-a-side legend Kurtice Herbert

02 The Cat, John Barnes and Sof – the start of a very good team

03 Another trophy haul for The Cat (one from right) and teammates

04 The Cat and company – well practiced in the post-tournament celebration pose

05 The Cat and his team-mates won a trip to Dubai

06 The Cat vs Cristiano. Ronaldo's nervous smile tells you he doesn't fancy his chances

Tales from the pitch

The Legend of the Hunter

By Neil Cotton

For over 10 years, a group of us have met every Thursday to play 5-a-side. Our group is of mixed ability, ranging from players, like myself, who never troubled the school team to guys who once played at regional or county level. Although the quality of these latter players is clear, they are never completely infallible, and can, with hard work, be contained. Steve Hunter, though, was different. His only weakness was the floppy fringe which sometimes got in his eyes and which he kept in check with a dab of water hastily applied pre-match. A colleague of one of the group's regulars – a car salesman – it was clear from the start that Hunter was the best we'd ever seen.

He had pace, control and strength. It was impossible to dispossess him and in full flow he would twist and turn, teasing the opposition, inviting tackles he'd skip away from, and playing solo one-twos with the side-boards. The display would only end when he became bored and shot. It always found the top corner. Alone he would be worth 15 to 20 goals for his team. I knew he'd been at Southern League side, Fleet Town, from the tracksuit he proudly wore each week. I later found out that he had once been involved with Fulham where he'd 'run rings' around the other players, but suffered from a lack of fitness.

Even the best of us posed little challenge, yet he returned week after week after week. Steve was a better footballer than a car salesman and his colleague informed us that he had been let go by his employers for not meeting his targets. He never returned to 5-a-side. This was many years ago. Just last week when warming up, two of us reminisced. "Remember that Steve Hunter?" I said. "Yeah, had a bloody shot on him didn't he?"

What Not To Wear

How much thought do you put into your 5-a-side kit? Steer away from these fashion disasters and you'll have a good chance of avoiding the ridicule of team-mates and opponents

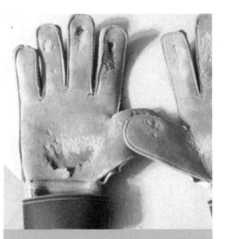

The smell of victory

The stench of unwashed kit can follow a player around like a poisonous cloud, alerting opponents to his every forward run like a kind of nausea-inducing Spidey sense. Putting your damp gear into your bag and keeping it in the back of your car until next week just isn't cool.

And can we please keep the bibs clean? You can boil wash your kit, shower, shave and dab on some Cool Water before kick-off, but if you're handed a crusty bib to play in, you're still going to smell like you slept in a skip.

See also:
radioactive goalie gloves

The antiques roadshow

To some players, it is more than a favourite kit, a lucky charm, a nostalgic nod to their favourite footballing era. This old top has become a part of their very being. We're not talking retro-cool, we're talking moth-eaten relic. It's time to retire this threadbare fossil of football's prehistory and update your on-pitch look.

See also: the undead trainers

The contender

Did I ever tell you that I once played for Blyth Spartans reserves? No? Well let me spare you the story by wearing the training kit they gave me, with my initials on and the name of the charming local car dealership that sponsored them back in '99, when I had the world at my feet. You know, before the injuries took it all from me.

Bare-chested brothers

With the summer heat comes the rare but unforgettably harrowing experience of playing against someone who whips off their top to proudly display the physique they have built up with countless hours in the gym and a series of dubious supplements purchased online.

Ever seen Ben Stiller get a face full of chest-sweat playing basketball against a Bare-chested Brother in Along Came Polly? That's what's coming your way.

Who loves short shorts?

Magic Johnson. That's not what they call him, that's what they call the thing perilously close to poking out of his scandalously short shorts. Hot pants looked great on Kylie, but that doesn't mean they are for everyone. Short is bad. Tight is bad. Short and tight makes you look like you're soliciting. Nobody wants to see your junk here. Inappropriate.

The rugby player

Talk about a fashion statement. Showing up to 5-a-side in rugby kit says a lot. Like, 'I am not a finesse player'. Or 'I place little value on the physical well-being of my opponent'. Expect awkward, robust (and by robust we mean illegal) tackles and over-cooked, toe-ended passes, all carried off with a big grin and a firm handshake.

See also: NFL; ice hockey; hurling

Blades of glory

In the quest to have the latest footwear, at some point, someone decided it was okay to wear blades to 5-a-side. It is not okay to wear blades to 5-a-side. In this fast, high-contact game people are going to stand on each other's feet. Without blades, this ends in the briefest of apologies and a tap on the shoulder. With blades, it ends with a broken metatarsal, five weeks out and a lifelong vendetta.

Save our Socks

The continental gentlemen may swan around the riviera wearing Corinthian leather loafers and no socks whilst retaining an air of carefree sophistication. Anyone who turns up at 5-a-side wearing no socks is, on the other hand, a disgrace.

Base-layer bandits

Base layers are great. Lightweight, comfortable and warm, there are a lot of benefits for athletes. However it's unlikely the original manufacturers had in mind that grossly-overweight men were going to be squeezing themselves into these garments in the same way that a butcher stuffs meat into his sausage skins. These are not corsets, people.

Head-bandits

Are you Socrates, the medically-trained, 6ft 4ins, chain-smoking captain of Brazil's legendary 1982 World Cup team? No? Then put that headband away, sir.

The king of bling

As far as we are aware, Mr T never played a single game of 5-a-side football, and for good reason too. The sheer quantity of jewellery would not only have made him far too slow, but it would've made him a prime target for locker room theft as well. Seriously though kids, there's no reason to wear jewellery to 5-a-side and rings can actually leave you with very, very nasty injuries.

Robocop

Okay, so there are probably some situations where a degree of support may be necessary to reduce the stress on a previously injured knee or ankle. However, we're going to need to see your doctor's note.

The double knee-support? The monumental ankle scaffolding? Are we playing 5-a-side or is this some weird MMA thing? What are you, Robocop?

Tales from the pitch

No Hollywood Ending

By Brian Jenkins

I used to go play pick-up soccer in Center City, Philadelphia. The rules were simple – 10-minute games or first goal wins. Winner stays on. It made for some intense attacking games. There were people out until midnight six nights a week all summer long. I was one of only a small handful of Americans that played. The South and Latin Americans were well represented, and there were lots of Italians, Turks, Greeks and Africans. Arguments would often start in more languages than I could keep up with.

Most nights I would go out with a buddy or by myself and see who needed a player. Some nights, when we were able to rouse enough people, we'd show up with a full team. We would rarely lose. We'd stay on all night and go home drenched in sweat.

At some point, a guy organized a National Urban Soccer tournament. Looking back now, the dude was shady. The tournament seemed legit though. It would be taking place in all major cities in the US and each city winner would go to LA to play in a final tournament at the Home Depot Center. We won the Philly tournament, so were headed for LA. The first sign of trouble was when we had to pay our own way, and then the travel agency went out of business.

When we got to LA, it turned out we weren't playing at the Home Depot Center. We were playing at a high school in Compton. The field was sandy with lots of broken glass. Our first match was at 8:30am. When we arrived there was a DJ spinning records. The refs didn't show up until after 11am. By this point, we were sure we were going to win. We got crushed – losing all three games easily! The tournament may have been a mess, but those guys could play.

Barnes
v
Lineker

5-a-side
Dream Team

Our Verdict – Lineker win

Tight game decided by Beardsley,
a striker tailor-made for 5-a-side

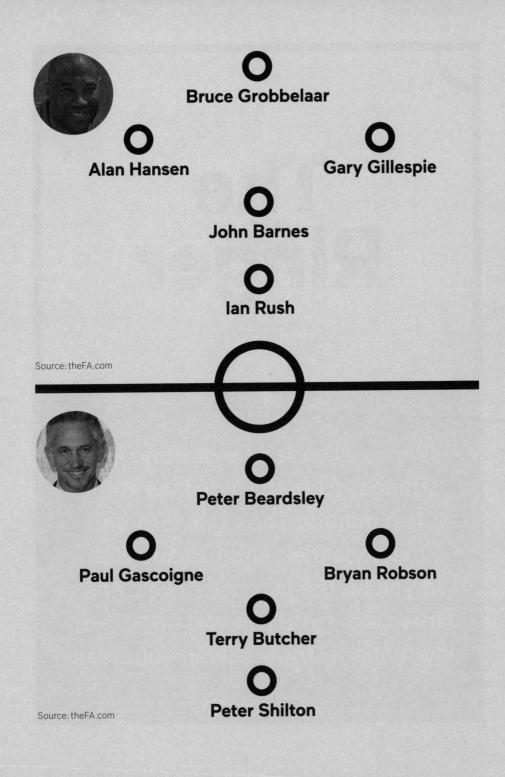

Bruce Grobbelaar

Alan Hansen

Gary Gillespie

John Barnes

Ian Rush

Source: theFA.com

Peter Beardsley

Paul Gascoigne

Bryan Robson

Terry Butcher

Peter Shilton

Source: theFA.com

The Ringer

We've all ended up drafting in a stranger from the sidelines at the last minute. Their talent rarely matches their enthusiasm. But if you hit the jackpot – like Chris Bruce did – you can end up with an international footballer in your team

Gavin McCallum – 'No, I don't want to go in goals.'

We used to play in a league and were a fairly average team. But we were pretty well liked by the other teams – or at least we thought so – and most importantly the organiser and referee liked us.

One evening we turned up with a full complement of five players and began performing a characteristically shambolic warm-up before the match. The ref came over and asked us if we wanted an extra player. "Don't think so ref, we're okay this week." Leaning in, the referee said: "Trust me lads, you want an extra guy."

Alright, we thought. Go on then.

Our new signing was called Gavin. We had already called on a few extras that season and none of them turned out to be much good. This one was Canadian, and without being too judgmental, they're not known for their rich production line of top footballers. So hopes weren't high.

"Oi mate, do you want to go in goal?" said one of our boys.

A simple "Nah" and a look of disgust was the reply.

"Where do you fancy playing?"

"I'll go up front," he said.

Predictable. The majority of ringers we had been given that season wanted to play the glory hunter, peppering the back boarding with wayward shots and refusing to track back. It's that sort of bastardry that's the reason most of them don't have their own team in the first place.

The game kicked off and within about 20 seconds our new man had smashed in his debut goal. Bosh. A minute later he'd got a second, and a third, then a fourth quickly after. It went very quickly into double figures. It was becoming a massacre out there. Eventually we had to sub him off just to give the opposition a chance. Whilst he wasn't outrageously skilful, it was his unbelievable acceleration and clinical finishing that was killing them.

At the end of the game we all knew we'd seen something a bit special. I asked him where he'd played. You don't see many players that good just loitering around desperate to join a team of strangers for some 5-a-side.

Turns out he'd been released by Lincoln and was in the area looking for another club. 5-a-side was his way of getting some match fitness to keep him sharp enough for any upcoming trials.

That night I went home and searched for our ringer on the internet. Lo and behold he had played for Lincoln as a forward and winger, and a load of other clubs too, but it also turned out that he'd made a full international appearance for the Canadian national team, scoring in a friendly against Venezuela.

When I told the other lads they were as amazed as I was that we'd had the chance to play with him. The amazement turned to laughter as we thought back to my mate offering him the chance to play in goal for us.

One day you're making your international debut for Canada, then a few short years later you're being asked if you want to play in goal for a ropey 5-a-side team. I imagine that was the low point of his career.

The Ultimate Ringer

Name: Gavin McCallum

Position: Striker. Not goalkeeper

Current club: Eastbourne Borough

Former clubs: Yeovil Town, Weymouth, Havant and Waterlooville, Sutton United, Hereford United, Lincoln City, Woking

Caps: One for Canada. McCallum made a scoring debut against Venezuela in a 1-1 draw on May 20, 2010

5-a-side
v
11-a-side

Why has fives eclipsed the full game as a participation sport? We examine the many reasons behind the revolution

Is 5-a-side really better than 11-a-side? Anyone who has played both will know that at times they are so different as to be like two distinct sports.

One thing we can say for certain is that 5-a-side is now more popular in terms of participation levels. But let's look at the reasons why the 5-a-side game is dominating...

More touches, more skills
5-a-side gives us a lot more touches than 11s, and more chance to display our silky skills on the pitch. Surely that's what football is supposed to be all about?

Playing in a smaller space and with fewer players, you're never far from the action. Whilst there might be potential for a hungover Sunday-league player to sheepishly hide away at left-back for a full 90 minutes, in 11-a-side you're going to be fully involved in a game of fives.

A FIFA study comparing 11-a-side to small-sided versions of the game found that in 4-a-side players get five times more touches than 11-a-side, whilst 7-a-side produces twice as many touches than 11-a-side. Another study found that players get over four times as many touches in 60 minutes of 5-a-side as they got in a full 90-minute game of 11-a-side football.

The ball spends less time out of play
Touch, pass, *throw-in*. Pass, tackle, *throw-in*. Dribble, shot, *goal-kick*.

That's a bit how 11-a-side can feel at times, with the ball spending a lot of time out of play followed by a set-piece. In fact, FIFA found that the ball is out of play for a whopping 34% of the time in 11-a-side.

If you're playing 5-a-side with barriers around the pitch then it goes out precisely 0% of the time. Without all those stoppages, 5-a-side is a more intense experience – and a better workout.

Better for fitness

Playing 5-a-side is scientifically proven to be more effective in reducing blood pressure, body fat, lowering cholesterol levels and improving aerobic fitness than other forms of exercise – including 11-a-side, cycling and swimming. It is also runs less risk of injury than 11-a-side.

Better facilities

When it comes to amateur football there's no debate – the facilities on offer to 5-a-side players are far superior to the 11-a-side game.

Who really wants to play on a muddy, dog-fouled quagmire when instead you could be playing on luscious synthetic 3G facilities?

The superb consistency of the pitches is a major reason why the 5-a-side game is suited to playing passes along the ground and skills, whilst 11s is often more suited to Peter Kay-esque punts: 'AVE IT!

5-a-side Vs 11-a-side

What's more, the facilities are all well-lit for evening football and many of them have a bar on the premises too, allowing us to enjoy a swift pint of 'sports drink' with team-mates after the game.

Less dependent on weather
The only time that your 5-a-side might get called off due to the adverse weather is when snow has literally covered the pitch. Flooding and freezing – the two most common causes for postponements on grass – do not apply here.

No seasons, no breaks
5-a-side keeps going throughout the summer months, which are the best times to be playing – there's nothing like getting your 5-a-side fix in the warm summer evenings.

11-a-side, on the other hand, shuts down for the off-season. This might be when the pros go on holiday and work on securing big transfer moves, but for the rest of us it's just a time to go steadily more deranged at the lack of footballing action.

5-a-side Vs 11-a-side

Thankfully, 5-a-side leagues run all year round making sure we don't ever have to spend some time apart from the game we love.

What's more, a 5-a-side 'season' usually only lasts a couple of months meaning that you can become a champion over and over... or, if things aren't going so well, you get more chances to wipe the slate clean.

More convenient and easier to organise

In the UK we are now spoiled for choice in terms of 5-a-side providers – most urban dwellers will be no more than five miles from a league near them.

It's quite possible to start a 5-a-side team and get it playing in competitive games within two weeks. The same cannot be said for 11-a-side.

Competitions and tournaments are readily available and you only need to round up four mates to get started. It might still feel like hard work rounding up a squad of five players at times, but be thankful that you're not trying to find a team of 11.

> A 5-a-side 'season' usually only lasts a couple of months meaning that you can become a champion over and over...

Numbers Game

Of the data available, it is easier to focus first on participation levels in England. According to the English Football Association's website:

Small-sided football is the most popular and fastest growing area of adult football. With over **1.5m adults** playing small-sided football every week and with **30,000 teams** playing in organised and competitive small-sided leagues, this format of football has increasingly become an integral part of the football family.

5-a-side is by far the most popular of a number of games which the English FA term "small-sided football". According to the FA, this label covers any version of the game played with less than 11 players. Most prominent in the small-sided category are the 5, 6 and 7-a-side games as well as Futsal and Beach Soccer. 1.5m is a vast number, but there is reason to believe that there are a lot more players out there since:

The FA's number is just the head count of players playing every week. The total number of players each year should be a lot higher.

The FA are only counting adults – children also play 5-a-side.

FA data suggests that only 16% of adult players play in organised competitions – the rest are just playing with their mates

If participation levels are consistent across the other parts of the UK, that number rises by 239,000

Of the two biggest 5-a-side centres in the UK, Goals have **130,000 players per week;** Powerleague have **560,000 players per month**

Tales from the pitch

Big Gav

By Jim Pervis

When I was at university we entered a 5-a-side team in the Intramural league. We steamrollered the opposition until the final game. That was the big showdown with our arch rivals, modestly named 'We Are It'. We were 'Five Bellies'.

A couple of hours before the game, our star striker called off with food poisoning. "Don't worry," he said, between bouts of spewing. "My flat-mate big Gav will play. He's more of a rugby man, but he's fit." And so big Gav turned up in full rugby kit. Our spewing striker was wrong. Big Gav wasn't 'more of a rugby man' – he was entirely a rugby man. He wasn't dirty. He just had a habit of running into people.

Five minutes into the match, he ploughed through their star man in a challenge that no one would have batted an eyelid at on the rugby pitch, but had us all wincing. The guy was immediately subbed and could be spotted on the sideline staring at his stricken limb in a state of shock. With the sub's first touch of the ball, big Gav struck again, charging him into the side-boards. He was also carried off, back to where he had came from moments earlier. It was now 4 v 5 and the game was still goalless.

We couldn't find a way through our battle-scarred opponents until the last five minutes when the ball landed at big Gav's feet six yards from goal. He drew his leg back – as if sizing up a conversion from the halfway line – and let fly. The ball crashed off the junction of the post and bar with such power that the goalframe came apart. The falling bar hit their goalkeeper on the back as nuts and bolts flew everywhere. The referee immediately blew the final whistle. "Match abandoned, lads. You can share the trophy. I'm getting out of here for my own safety." Big Gav nodded quietly and headed for the showers, leaving a scene resembling a hospital ward in his wake.

Anger Management

How to tame the beast inside

We all know him – the mild-mannered mate who turns into a homicidal maniac on the fives pitch. Here are some tips on how to chill out and actually enjoy the game

Picture the scene: It's a Wednesday night, you've gone to the movies with your friends. You've been looking forward to seeing the latest blockbuster all week but on the way in you get less-than-satisfactory customer service from the cashier. It's the snack vendor's first day and he takes ages to get your popcorn. Then, to top it all off, one of your friends sits in the seat you really wanted.

You've got two ways to deal with this scenario: a) accept it for what it is, a series of unfortunate events which you're not going to let ruin your trip to the movies. Or b) totally freak out, swear at the cashier, gear up for physical violence against some complete strangers and generally ruin the experience for yourself, your friends and your fellow cinephiles.

Nearly everyone would like to go for option (a) because option (b) represents the behaviour of a deplorable monster.

Of course it would seem crazy to flip out over a few small inconveniences, but anyone who has played football has witnessed crazy reactions to fairly trivial things on the field of play, and some of us have even been the perpetrators.

Why are you getting angry about a game of football?
You might take issue with the previous example. Going to the movies can't be compared to a game of football – it doesn't have any of the same pressures or levels of testosterone in the atmosphere.

However, your weekly game of football is one of your main recreational activities so you should view it like any other – don't ruin it for yourself or others by temporarily letting go of your sanity. Remember, you're choosing to play football rather than do something else, so you should enjoy it. Just like going to the movies, you're spending time with friends, and paying your hard-earned cash to do so – shouldn't you be enjoying it rather than going mental?

Bob Marley – 'Let's get together and feel alright.'

When people look at it in detached, rational terms, it's hard to explain exactly why they get so angry on the pitch. In the heat of battle it's not so easy to think in such a clear way and the mercury can rise very quickly on your anger thermometer if you don't keep a sense of perspective.

Try the following to help you keep calm and enjoy your football.

1. Get to know people

Get to know your own team-mates, the referees and other players and you'll realise that generally they're all normal guys who, like you, are just looking to have some fun playing football.

It's not as hard as you think it would be to get to know loads of people quite quickly. The odd bit of banter with the referee, or some talk with other teams about how their season is going can open up plenty of conversation and you'll get to know people if you consistently keep this effort up over a period of time.

Knowing people will count for a lot – it'll help you stop seeing them as the 'enemy' and in turn, they'll come to see you as a good guy too.

Bob Marley had it about right when he sang: "Let's get together and feel all right." Making the effort to know and understand other people will help you keep your cool. Bob also loved a game of football and once told a journalist: 'If you want to get to know me, you have to play football against me and The Wailers.'

2. Face the truth

A lot of the stress of sport comes from the expectations we set ourselves about the game we're playing. A good number of these expectations are unrealistic.

If every player could accept the following, there would be a lot less aggravation on the football field:

> Whether you've won or lost, it's not going to make any difference to your life. It's more important to be pleased with having put in an honest level of effort.

> It won't make you any less of a person if you have a bad game. A bad game is your feedback on what you need to improve next time.

> Everyone around you makes mistakes: your team-mates, the opposition, the referee and you – nobody is perfect, nor does anybody purposely try to make mistakes, so cut them some slack.

> Somebody's lack of skill is down to a lack of talent or practice. Getting angry with them won't fix their problems.

> You are a free-thinking individual – the attitude of others does not need to determine your own attitude. You, not anybody else, are responsible for the way you think and behave.

Leave justice in the hands of the referee – they're trying their best, and abusing them is not going to help them or you. Shake the referee's hand when you leave the field of play.

In sport and in life in general, things aren't always fair. The best man doesn't always come out on top, but being angry about it is not a constructive response.

3. Communicate

Bottling your frustrations can often lead to an explosion of emotions, resulting in losing your temper at some point down the line.

Don't let an issue fester and eat away at you. Try to communicate a problem to others in a calm, clear and constructive way. If it's put in a way that helps them, others will often be glad to know what they can do to fix a problem.

4. Channel your anger

Sometimes it's hard not to feel angry, but we don't always have to express it in a negative way. Anger is an energy that can be channelled into constructive thoughts. It can improve our focus and inspire extra effort. Try to use your anger and frustration to improve your own performance without it spilling over to others.

5. The bottom line – get a grip

Anger will ruin your sporting experience and, worse still, can turn other people away from the game. Few people turn up to play sports with the hope or expectation of violent confrontation.

Some players like Roy Keane might have played on the edge all the time but, let's face it, who would really want to play 5-a-side with him every week? Keep a lid on it people, take control of yourselves and enjoy your football.

Anger will ruin your sporting experience and, worse still, can turn other people away from the game

Emperor Palpatine – 'Use your aggressive feelings, boy!'

Confessions of a Referee

We asked one anonymous official
what it's like to be all alone
inside the cage

The referee. While a lot of our games don't need him, when things get serious, he becomes an essential part of 5-a-side. But what is the game like viewed through the eyes of the solitary match official, whose job it is to make instant decisions on the blur of action in front of him – and to put up with all of our moaning?

Here's the inside track from a referee who's been on the front line of fives and lived to tell the tale.

How do you handle things as a 5-a-side referee?

Even in the difficult tournaments where you get the so-called 'rowdy' teams coming from far and wide, you've just got to be authoritative. If you're just going to act timid and let them shout at you, they're going to keep doing it. If you say 'do that again and I'll send you off', or sin-bin them, then they'll either quieten down or when you send them off they'll come back on and won't do it again.

Why does somebody who is calm by day turn into an idiot by night, when it comes to 5-a-side?

It's just like that with football in general, but 5-a-side is played in small spaces which creates havoc. It doesn't take a lot to get into a tackle and then before you know it you're angry. Also it's a way for people to take out their stress.

People say it's not all about the winning, but as soon as you get out there in the cage and you're losing 3-0 you start to care about winning. It's competitive. When you're losing you get even more frustrated.

You find the worse the standard of the league, the friendlier it is. The better the standard, the closer the games and the more intense it gets. The better players seem to care about losing more because it hurts their pride.

When you have the big tournaments that bring the best players together, there are many more fights, arguments and sendings off. They're all used to winning at their own venues and can't accept things going against them.

What is the one message you'd send from a referee to a player?
You are never ever as right as you think you are! There are some fouls that you look at and think 'how are you even arguing with me about it?' Somebody goes straight through the back of someone, takes them out and says 'I've barely touched him', although they've almost broken his legs.

Try to put yourselves in the ref's shoes. Some players do have an attitude that they don't need to respect the referees; that referees are guys who have never played the game themselves and don't understand it. I play in a 7-a-side team and we're the league winners, and that does seem to help me get a bit of extra respect from the players. They know I play.

You hear people saying 'you don't know anything about football, you've probably never kicked a ball in your life', so many times on the pitch. And a lot of referees haven't, to be fair. But it still doesn't make a difference.

What do you think of the different rules used in 5-a-side?
We play using the head-height rule. Everyone disputes this rule so we recently had a white line put up (at 6ft) behind the goal, so that everyone understands exactly what height this is. We always get one or two people saying 'but his head is over 6ft' but now I can just say 'no, shut up, it's that line, end of story'.

With the area rule [where you can't go in the area], people do argue about it, but if you got rid of it, you'd probably get a lot more clashes between goalkeepers and outfield players.

Legends
of
5-a-side

A fat lad with decent feet

Rejected by Stockport County, Stuart Cook found the perfect platform for his talents in fives and later futsal, where he represented England

Speaking to Stuart Cook, it's a big surprise to learn that he was not always the skills machine that flip-flaps his way through the competition as if they were training dummies. His big move was only developed after he moved into 5-a-side, and was inspired by his hero, Ronaldinho.

Less surprisingly, more depressingly, he was cut loose by one Championship team and rejected by two other clubs, because of his lack of height, not his ability. Moving to 5-a-side increased his skill levels. And he got taller. Because that's what really short teenagers do, eventually.

The self-assessment as 'a fat lad with decent feet' is not exactly correct. You don't get dozens of England futsal caps if you're a porker, and his feet are way better than decent.

What was your story as a young footballer?
I was born in 1986 and, as a youngster I was involved in academy teams. At 16 I was in my final year as a schoolboy with Stockport County, who were in the Championship.

I was only about 4ft 8 at the time, but they offered me a one-year contract on the Youth Training Scheme around Christmas of that year to see if I would develop physically. But at the end of the season the chairman sold the club and there was a big turnover in the coaching staff so they didn't pick me up. I had a couple of trials at Bolton and Crewe, but they all said the same thing: I was too small to take a chance on.

After leaving Stockport I went from being about 4'10 to 5'9 in about 12 months – eventually growing to just under 6 feet! I had a few growing pains so didn't play a lot in that period, but after a while I found my way into semi-pro football, picking up £100 per week. That was all the money I needed in the world at that age; I was enjoying life and it never really occurred to me to get another club.

How did you get into 5-a-side?

It was around that time that I also started playing 5-a-side because a few of my mates were playing, and it had a good social side to it.

I had no interest in trying to get back into the 11-a-side game. I had a proper job, plus I was really enjoying 5-a-side: it was giving me more touches on the ball and more enjoyment. I just found that it suited me a little bit more.

From age 17 to 20 I played 5-a-side almost every night of the week with different sets of mates in different areas.

So, how good were you when you first started?

I wasn't particularly skilful as a player at age 15 or 16. I was more a sort of pass-tackle-move-head player, just looking to do the basics right as a central midfielder. I had always been brought up the right way by my Dad; I was never a natural athlete so my best chance to make it was to be a better footballer than most. I could do all the basics with both feet which I still try to keep up even now.

Then as soon as I moved to 5-a-side I just started picking things up. My favourite player at the time was Ronaldinho and I watched a couple of videos of him and tried to copy his skills. Luckily the videos seemed to work and things went from there.

Having seen videos of you playing later on, it seems difficult to believe you weren't very skilful!

I wasn't. I had tidy feet and I could do a decent Cruyff turn, and I could get myself out of a little bit of trouble, but I'm not quick and I never have been. In the 11-a-side game I was never a dribbler; when I got the ball it was a case of take a touch and find a pass.

It's only when I started playing 5-a-side that I thought, 'this might work here, and that might work there'. If you put yourself in these situations often enough, you pick skills up and it just becomes natural. I've always said I'm not a great dribbler, but if the ball drops between me and three other people, however it happens, I end up on the other side with the ball. My feet have done the work and I haven't even thought about it.

My favourite player at the time was Ronaldinho and I watched a couple of videos of him and tried to copy his skills

Nowadays it seems to come naturally to me in tight situations. But I think it's because I played so much 5-a-side. I spent three years just picking the ball up off my goalkeeper, running into three defenders and ending up out on the other side of them.

What were your high points in 5-a-side?

It was only really towards age 20 that I started playing in big tournaments. Myself and a friend started a team called FC Fodder down in Stockport Powerleague.

We were all good footballing lads but when we used to play the other teams in the major tournaments they always seemed to have one big guy at the back who just used to kick us. We always struggled with it, and even if we outplayed them we'd go out on penalties having bottled it. We called ourselves 'Semi Final FC'.

But we did have a few good wins: the best one was winning the Nike Fives in 2009. They'd put a lot of money into the venues and the organisation, converting Alexandra Palace for a crowd of around 1000 people watching. It wasn't all about winning though. It has always been about having fun with mates – oh and keeping my reputation intact.

So things were going well, what happened next?

At the start of 2010 I had a badly injured knee. At first, nobody was exactly sure what I'd done and I spent a couple of months trying to see physios and strengthen it up a little. Stupidly I was still playing on it every now and then because I missed 5-a-side so much.

Eventually I got an MRI scan and they told me that I had torn my ACL and that I had cartilage damage. I had three operations with the final one being an ACL reconstruction. It took me around 15 months to play football again.

You're well known now for your involvement in futsal, with Manchester Futsal Club and England. Tell us about how that came about...

The England futsal team were looking for some more technical players than the ones who were already playing. This was around the time when I had been playing in a lot of 5-a-side tournaments. The FA's head of small-sided football did a lot of scouting around and they picked several of us players up from the traditional 5-a-side game, including Rob Ursell (see p190).

In my first games of futsal for England I wasn't even sure of the rules. I didn't play club futsal until four or five months later. It's a very different game and at the time I didn't realise quite how different it was.

I just wanted to get the ball and dribble like I do in traditional 5-a-side. Futsal is a lot more competitive than traditional 5-a-side, a lot more of a challenge. In normal 5-a-side I'm only ever marked by one person but in futsal it's at least one and a half, if not two defenders because everyone is covering each other. You really have to work hard to find a dribbling opportunity.

In my experience, a lot of the players who play traditional 5-a-side have got more ability than the futsal players, but they don't seem to have the mental attributes to deal with the tactics and organisation of futsal.

Before my knee operation I had played six games for England's futsal team. It took me about two-and-a-half years to return to playing for them but now I'm closing in on 50 caps and have enjoyed some great trips travelling the world. There have been some experiences I'll never forget: I mean, how many people can say they've been into Colonel Gaddafi's house after beating Libya – who were the African champions – in their own back yard.

Most of my football these days is played with Manchester Futsal Club. It's full of great people and I can say I have met most of my best mates through them. It's a real family club and everyone strives to keep us at the top of English futsal both on and off the court. Working with youngsters is great and I love visiting our development centres and trying to pass on bits of knowledge to the kids.

The Manchester futsal lads still play traditional 5-a-side from time to time. I enjoy both traditional 5-a-side and futsal because I get loads of touches on the ball. 11-a-side is great for the competitive edge, the fitness, the running around, but what I want to do is have the ball at my feet and be looking to score a goal, beat someone, 'meg someone and make them think 'he's a decent player for a fat lad'. 5-a-side lets me do that.

What position do you play?
I started off as a pivot (the attacker at the top of the formation) but now I play as the back man or fixo. I have found that you can have so much more influence on the game from that position.

You're often the one starting the attacks, and I consider that I read the game well so I can help other people out by covering them. When I play futsal I'm the loudest player on the pitch.

Playing 5-a-side it's important that you're there to help everyone. In 11-a-side you can get a bit lost in the game: you can't do everyone's job for them. But in 5-a-side and futsal constantly talking can make the difference, closing up the middle, offering people help and knowing that if your team-mates get beaten you can make the distance up and cover them.

Stuart Cook's top tips for 5-a-side

no.1

Be effective rather than flashy

I've got good feet, but I never try to over-complicate it. I learned to do a right footed flip-flap playing 5-a-side and nobody could ever stop it, so I just used it all the time. I never tried to get too flashy with it. The only thing I've done since is to learn to do it on my left foot, and it works. Find what works for you as an individual and use it.

no.2

Shoot!

Some of the younger lads I play with at the moment overplay so much. When you're playing 5-a-side and you get half a yard of space within 15-20 yards of goal just put it in the corner. Find that half a yard and hit the bottom corner, there's no sweeter feeling.

no.3

Have fun!

I've seen guys who can't have any fun when they play because they're getting so frustrated with themselves when they make a mistake. You can really underestimate how much having fun affects your game. Most of the time when you're there playing 5-a-side it's because you want to be there, so go out and enjoy it and don't be afraid to express yourself.

no.4

Defend well and communicate

Defending well and communication are the key aspects of winning. Communication is the biggest factor in conceding goals. If you're constantly talking to each other, helping each other out, telling each other where your man is going and where somebody hasn't spotted a run, if you can see something they can't then you're giving them an advantage that they wouldn't have had otherwise.

Rakitic v Cole

5-a-side Dream Team

Our Verdict – Cole win

Despite the presence of Messi in Rakitic's line-up, Ashley Cole's powerhouse midfield axis of Vieira and Gerrard proves too strong and Henry nets the winner in a high-scoring contest

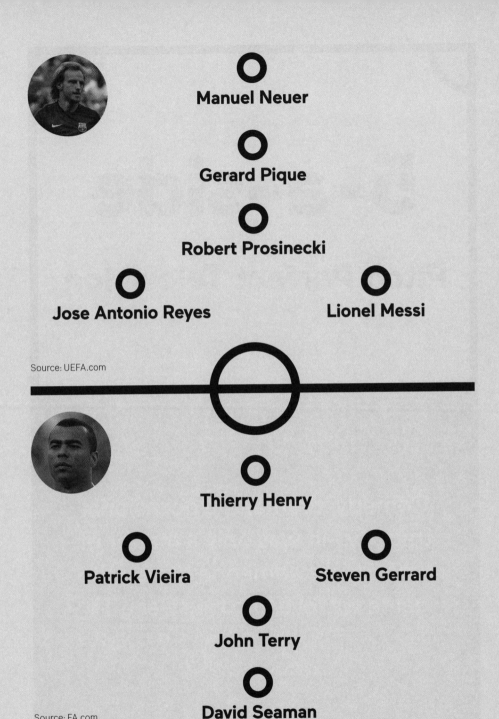

Manuel Neuer

Gerard Pique

Robert Prosinecki

Jose Antonio Reyes

Lionel Messi

Source: UEFA.com

Thierry Henry

Patrick Vieira

Steven Gerrard

John Terry

David Seaman

Source: FA.com

5-a-side

Pitch Perfect Television

Comedy, drama, the occasional tragedy – it was only a matter of time before someone turned the game we love into must-see TV

When two TV producers had the idea to make their version of Sex and the City for men they needed to find a vehicle – something their characters would love as much as Sarah Jessica Parker adores overpriced shoes. They chose 5-a-side. Of course they did.

Fittingly for a comedy-drama about the fastest growing form of football in the 21st Century, '5-a-side' is a thoroughly modern affair – a series of shorts that went straight to YouTube, on the channel of the production company, This is Drama.

Its stars include old and new media icons: former Boyzone crooner Keith Duffy and KSI, a YouTuber with a fanatical following for his gaming videos. Those two – along with Michael Nardone,

Ceallach Spellman and Paul Sculfor – play members of a 5-a-side team with whom we can all identify, to some extent at least.

We caught up with Aileen Docherty, one of the creators of the show, to ask why she wrote about 5-a-side and the huge response the show has received.

What got you interested in this subject for a comedy-drama?

Aileen: Sex and the City is a bunch of girls talking to each other over cocktails in New York. Where do guys talk to each other? On the pitch, the changing room and the pub. In drama we don't tend to see that side of things. It's never been done before. I've got two brothers and a husband who I've watched playing 5-a-side. My nine-year-old son plays in a Monday tournament every week and it is the biggest thing in his week. It's an amazing sport, so competitive.

Men's frustrations come out in 5-a-side. The five actors in the series bonded beyond belief. It was an eclectic mix of people you would never put together. We put them up against freestylers and extras. They become a well-formed group of friends. The big thing was that we wanted the football to be realistic. All five actors played 5-a-side and when they played it in the series, they played it for real. Keith Duffy plays fives every week with his son.

By the final game in the series, they were all saying 'We'll bring them down!'

How did you find working with KSI, who is well known for a different kind of content?

His character was quite true to who he is. YouTubers are good to work with because they speak to the camera two or three times a week. They've not been drama trained but they've also not picked up the bad habits. Michael Nardone took him under his wing. KSI had a great work ethic and when we were filming down at Powerleague, he was mobbed.

Nobody asked any of the other famous actors for autographs, and in the end we had to bring in security.

What was the response like when you aired on YouTube?

Two days after we put it out we had 1.5million hits. Sky launched their premium drama the same night and got 250,000. We're doing what we're doing because the landscape is changing.

To watch 5ASIDE the series and future series – go to ThisIsDrama on YouTube – youtube.com/user/ThisIsDRAMA

Michael Nardone (Nick, far left): "I hadn't played football in ages before the show – I just get to play the old guys now!"

Keith Duffy (Johnny, second left): "I'm surprised the concept of 5-a-side football hasn't been put into a movie or a TV show before now."

KSI (Matt, centre): "My agent told me to check it out – I'd never done acting before. It's a drama, but it's funny, too."

Ceallach Spellman (Lee, second right): "The script's great – it's more than just the 5-a-side, it's everything that's going on around it."

Paul Sculfor (Lee, far right): "My character's a bit of a cheeky chap – loves women, loves cars, adores football. He's a fun guy."

KSI – Football-loving YouTube phenomenon

Tales from the pitch

Thou Shalt Not Pass

By Rosco McIntosh

We play 5-a-side regularly and most of the time we have the same players, but every now and then, either through injuries or other commitments, we need replacements. One time we had a new guy come in and play. He was late 20s, left footed and seemed a decent standard, so all looked good.

Anyway, weeks went on and we noticed that this guy never passed if you were on his right-hand side, the ball always went left or he lost it. We put it down to the fact he was new.

We are quite a mellow, easy-going lot but this was starting to get to us all. So it was agreed that if it continued someone would have to tell him to stop being a greedy bollocks and pass, or we would need to get someone else.

One week after it had happened again, we all agreed we would confront him and see what his problem was. Everyone was pumped and ready for confrontation when the player declared that he was deaf in one ear. Never have I seen a team of grown men so humbled.

The Fives Commandments

Rules of the Game

Slide tackles allowed? Head height? What about passbacks? Here's your definitive guide to the many variations in the 5-a-side rule book

You've been drafted in as a late replacement for a mate's game. You don't know anybody else. There's some stuff you need to work out. Not least why have you just been penalised for picking the ball up from a pass–back? Shouldn't that long pass have been called for head–height? And why is the guy who elbowed that dude in the face still on the pitch?

Football is football, but in 5-a-side there are enough rule variations to make it a good idea to always ask before you play somewhere for the first time.

What follows is not a comprehensive list – more a discussion of the rights and wrongs of some of the laws that can help and hinder your weekly game of 5-a-side.

The area of uncertainty
The off-limits nature of the D-shaped penalty box in 5-a-side seems to be a legacy rule. It's always been there and at this point nobody can remember where it came from, or why it persists.

But there it is. Touch the ball on the wrong side of that white line and you face a free-kick at best, maybe a penalty, and possibly a short prison term. In some games, the ball isn't even an issue – step into the D and it's all over for you.

The result is a strange kind of obsessive pedantry around this rule, with eagle-eyed law keepers more intent on calling opponents for a stray toe in the penalty box than marking their man. It can also give rise to some ugly wrestling around the D, a primal battle for the prime real estate just on the right side of legal. It's just not right.

What would happen if the rule was done away with? It's not as if we'd see attackers loitering on the goalline – the demands of 5-a-side just don't allow a team to carry players with such one-dimensional games.

Step into the D and it's all over for you

The safety of the goalkeeper would not be jeopardised – especially if the common outlawing of slide tackles was in place.

Instead, attacks could flow without this artificial boundary – there would be more passing options for attacking teams and more goals.

It's time to liberate the D.

Slide away

Almost all organised 5-a-side tournaments outlaw the slide tackle and it's probably a good thing. In competitive situations, with play moving quickly in a tight space, there are fewer situations when the slide tackle would be the right option. However, it's in a lot of players' DNA and the results can be dangerous.

A well-timed slide tackle is a thing of beauty – a player gracefully drifting across the floor to dink the ball away from danger whilst at full-stretch, making little or no contact with the opponent. But for every graceful Bobby Moore, there are a dozen reckless Vinnie Jones'. This is a rule that keeps standards up and protects the players. It's a good thing.

Never go back

Let's assume the penalty box is off limits. In that case, many games outlaw a back-pass from the player who receives the ball from the goalkeeper.

This is an interesting little rule that catches out many a 5-a-side newcomer. It offers concrete protection against the most blatant time-wasting tactic available to a team and increases the technical demands placed upon the player receiving the ball, which is a good thing.

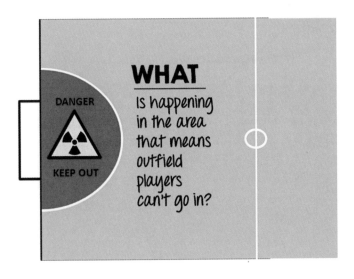

DANGER

KEEP OUT

WHAT is happening in the area that means outfield players can't go in?

However, let's get the other side of the rule right. A penalty should never be given as a result of a back-pass. Let's make the punishment fit the crime – the offender should concede possession, with an indirect free-kick, not a penalty.

The height of inconvenience

The rule which stops play when the ball goes above 'head height' is another from the old school that does not stand up to scrutiny.

First of all, it's a hard call to make. Sometimes it goes according to the tallest player on the pitch – fine if you're playing with Peter Crouch. More recently, some pitches have a white line on the boards to indicate the limit. Either way,

it can result in a lot of marginal calls and another area for pedantic spoilers to exploit.

The bigger question is: why do we need it? The idea behind it is surely to discourage the aimless long balls and desperate clearances that are common in Sunday League 11-a-side. But it also takes away a range of passes and finishes – deft chips, cushioned headers and volleyed passes – that are as skilful as anything that can be produced by playing the game entirely on the deck.

We think 5-a-side has already won the battle against the long ball – it's time to ditch this rule and add another element to your game.

Some centres use a 'head height' marker to reduce confusion.

It's a long shot
(but it just might work)

A common rule in social games – but less so in tournaments – outlaws any shots from the player's own half. The reason is to bring a little tiki-taka to your Wednesday night game. After all, where's the fun in the whole thing turning into long-range shooting practice?

Perhaps those kind of shots happen so rarely, and have so little success anyway, that it's a bit of an irrelevance, but at least this rule has its heart in the right place.

Corner-geddon

The sight of a football rolling into the corner of a 5-a-side pitch can do strange things to a man. Despite this being an area of comparable neutrality, it can turn the most disciplined defender into a raging bull and the most soft-shoed attacker into an elbows-out nut-job without peer. The result is something very much like a cage match taking place in the corner of your game of 5-a-side. Powerleague rules outlaw any contact by a defender when the attacker has the ball in the corner – and also forbids holding the boards, another key ingredient of Corner-geddon. Many social games have an unwritten rule that the attacker will be allowed to play the ball out – the defender can ensure the only option is a pass down the line and his team-mates can organise themselves for the play that will follow that pass.

No footballing good can come from Corner-geddon, and it can start a lot of trouble. It would be nice if we all realised this in our own time and moved on, but if you need to legislate for it, then maybe you should.

Hits it, gets it

Finally, one we can all agree on. You hit the ball over the fence, you better believe it's you who has to fetch it.

Legends of 5-a-side

King of Fives

Kurtice Herbert is the deadliest finisher on the circuit. He told us how he does it – and how you can too

Ask the elite 5-a-side players who is the greatest of all time, and the answer is the same: Sof. But in Sof's wake are a lot of other players aspiring to have the same impact he has had over the past two decades. And somewhere around the top of that list is one name: Kurtice Herbert.

One of the players that opponents would least like to see on the other side of the court, Kurtice is never far from the prize podium at any major tournament.

Anyone who has seen him play knows he has the talent to be a pro footballer, and he was in the system – from Premier League youth academy to non-league first-teamer – for long enough. But the system seems to have been the problem for Kurtice, and these days you are more

likely to find him banging in the goals at 5-a-side than playing the politics of the full game.

In many ways 5-a-side is the perfect home for Kurtice. His close control, mastery of space and ability to conjure up a killer finish from the tightest situation make him a matchwinner on the court, and few can match his record of tournament wins.

He's an interesting guy – willing to look back on what happened early in his career, and to analyse what he has learned in 5-a-side.

At Arsenal's training even the kids were playing 5-a-side. That's why they are so good at the passing game

Why aren't you playing pro?

I was once in the Fulham FC academy. I was there from age 8 to 15. Then at 15 I took a year out and left by mutual agreement because my brother passed away and at that point I needed to figure out what I wanted to do.

Whilst I was out, I ended up going on a trial version of a TV show called Football Icon. Out of 500 kids I got picked and went on trial in Chelsea's youth programme. One of the factors in me leaving Fulham was a coach who I didn't get on with at the time. Unbelivably, he turned up to work at Chelsea as my trial period was finishing – so that didn't help my chances of staying on.

I played 11-a-side for a lot of clubs: Harrow Borough, Edgware Town, Hendon, Southall and Hanwell Town, but as semi-pro there's too much politics. If you're not in the clique, if you don't want to go and have a drink with the boys, it's just hard. I haven't got time for all that.

Why did you start playing more 5-a-side?

I came to 5-a-side in 2009. When I was in the academies we didn't really play 5-a-side. You'd have 3-on-3 keep-ball sessions, but you'd never really have a game.

Funnily enough though, we went to Arsenal's training one day and even the kids were playing 5-a-side. That's why I think Arsenal are so good at the passing game. Where I was, it wasn't really about playing free football. They wanted you to have a good first touch, but the focus was more about getting down the wing and getting crosses in.

One of the reasons that I stopped playing 11-a-side and switched to 5-a-side and futsal is that even the semi-pro 11-a-side teams were all about getting the ball and hitting it into a target man. I'm not a player who just wants to chase flick-ons. I'm not a greyhound. There's no grass in the air, that's what my dad taught me. Most of the time you've got to play the ball on the floor.

01 A skills legend – and
    Cristiano Ronaldo

02 Kurt (third from left)
    celebrating with the aid
    of his injured IFC team-
    mate's crutches

02

Did you know immediately that you had found your game?

I wasn't as good at 5-a-side when I first started playing. I was a bit arrogant about it. I'd come up against tough teams and they'd be beating us 6- or 7-0. I was young and it just made me angry. I didn't realise that they were playing this one-touch stuff to draw us out so they could set it up for a goal. It wasn't until I started playing with good players that I started realising how it should be done.

All of the legends of 5-a-side are great players. When I was coming on to the scene, I watched Stuart Cook, Rob Ursell and Sof, and I've taken aspects of what they do and adapted it to my game. When I first started, I wasn't half the player I am now – it's only from looking at those guys, and other great players that I became the player I am today.

The best 5-a-side player ever, from what I've seen, is Sof. He does some amazing things, even now when he's into his 40s. I've always wanted to do his skills on the 5-a-side circuit. Everyone still talks about him, and he's been doing it for 20 years.

It took me about a year to really establish myself on the 5-a-side scene and for people to start talking about me as a decent player. We got to a national final in 2010 and lost, but that suddenly made me realise that we were up there with the best. Shortly after that we won the KIA tournament which sent us on a trip to South Africa and that inspired me to work harder.

When did you realise that you were starting to make a serious impact on the 5-a-side circuit?

I started seeing people's faces as I would get on the pitch and they'd look worried about who was going to mark me. In 2011 things exploded. We won the Wembley nationals and people were really talking about me and my team, Top Drawer. It's great that people respect what I do on the pitch. When I go to tournaments people come up to me and ask me for advice or say 'I've seen you on YouTube'. They even want to take pictures.

Often now when I'm playing I can see people watching and I feel as though I've got to turn the show on. Some people mistake that for me being cocky, but it's not – I just want to give the people watching something good to look at.

I love 5-a-side because it lets me do something that I'm good at. Even people who I play against have given me compliments. I like the competitiveness and even when I lose, I like it that there's other players out there who can become better than me and better than my team.

I like it when there's a buzz from the sides – when there have been people around the cage shouting 'do that again,' that's inspiring to me. Sometimes people think I'm big-headed, but I didn't get good at this game by just sitting around and doing nothing. I've worked hard, travelled up and down, I've sat underneath bridges where we've broken down on the way to tournaments, waiting three hours for someone to come and get us. I've sat on trains for six hours to get to tournaments, getting out of my bed at 4am. They don't see me standing in the pouring rain, waiting for a bus just to get to a game. I've got the confidence to play the game, but I've had to work to get decent at it.

And what are your biggest wins?

As well as the South Africa trip I've been to Lisbon and met Cristiano Ronaldo. I've had trips to Dubai, Singapore, Poland and Ukraine. Recently we won a £6000 cash prize. I've won plenty of national tournaments. We've also played against pros as a result of winning some tournaments. In Poland we played a match against Patrik Berger, Míchel Salgado, Nuno Valente, Vítor Baía and Bolo Zenden.

We also once played against a team of street footballers that Edgar Davids put together. That was when I had just started and we were very young. I got outrageously nutmegged on camera by one of those guys. People sometimes wind me up about that happening, but I took that nutmeg from him and I use the same skill now on other people.

We won a £6000 cash prize. I've won plenty of national tournaments

Play it on the deck

He maybe the deadliest finisher on the 5-a-side circuit but Kurtice Herbert is also a purist. He claims that keeping the ball low is vital to fives success.

'One of the reasons that I stopped playing 11-a-side and switched to 5-a-side and futsal is that even the semi-pro 11-a-side teams were all about getting the ball and hitting it into a target man. I'm not a player who just wants to chase flick-ons. I'm not a greyhound. There's no grass in the air, that's what my dad taught me. Most of the time you've got to play the ball on the floor'

I've won things playing for lots of different teams. When I first started, it was with a team called Hammersmith and Fulham, but the team I had most success with were called Top Drawer. If my team doesn't get through in a tournament, I often get asked to go and play for other teams – it's a good opportunity to win things, but those teams also know that if I'm not playing for them I'll be playing against them for someone else.

Kurtice's Tactics Board

Keep the Ball: 5-a-side is a game where you need to keep your head. It's also a game where it's vital to keep the ball. Like the saying goes, if you've got the ball then the opposition can't score. Especially if you're a goal up, if you can keep the ball then you're sorted.

Be Direct: I've always played as the furthest player forward, we call it the 'top man'. When I first started playing, I would get in front of goal and then pass it off. In 5-a-side sometimes it's better to take that opportunity yourself. When I first started playing 5-a-side I was more about passing, then doing a skill, then passing again. Now I try to be more focused on being direct and getting shots off.

Get behind the ball: We used to mark man-for man, so the middle was always open. Guys who know 5-a-side generally use the 'experienced' set-up **(opposite)**. When we first came into it we were getting beaten by pub teams and guys with big bellies. We were coming off the pitch saying "look at the size of them", but all they were doing was using simple tactics where they'd give it to the top man who was a big hefty guy who would just stick the ball in the net. A good 5-a-side team does the basics well, and if you do that you've got a good chance of winning.

Beginners

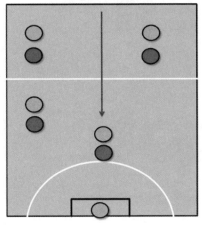

Experienced

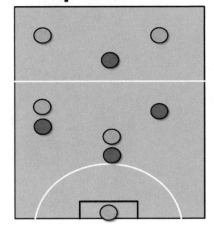

Going man-for-man like this was how we started. But this leaves the middle open and if the ball gets to their top man then he's got three runners – Very hard to defend!

Now we play the diamond, where you have a guy stopping them going down the middle. Their two defenders can have the ball and go back and forth between them, but they have to try to break the diamond

Owen
v
Walcott

5-a-side
Dream Team

Our Verdict – Owen win

Close contest, but the quick feet
of Zidane and Ronaldo provide the
greater firepower

O

Edwin van der Sar

O

Rio Ferdinand

O

Steven Gerrard

O

Zinedine Zidane

O

Ronaldo
(The Brazilian one)

O

Thierry Henry

O

Wayne Rooney

O

David Beckham

O

Ashley Cole

O

Jens Lehmann

What do you mean 'You can't play?'

Short of cash? Watching the kids? Leg hanging off? It's never okay to leave your team-mates in the lurch

There are very, very few acceptable excuses for pulling out of 5-a-side. Death – your own, not a family member – is one, but just about anything else is unacceptable.

And the only thing that's worse than the call-off, is the late call-off. Pulling out on the day of the game is the most heinous of crimes. There are repeat offenders in every game and they should know we are onto them.

The No-Show

The game has started but the 10th man hasn't turned up. Everyone keeps glancing forlornly towards the car park, hoping for his imminent arrival. 15 minutes into a one-sided 5 v 4 game, the organiser digs out his mobile phone and calls 'the no-show'. It rings out. The game ends with a 22-goal win for the team with five players. Everyone goes home disappointed.

Sample text message:
"Just saw your missed call. Was the game tonight?!"

The No-Excuse

It's bad enough pulling out, but when you don't even have the decency to make up a decent excuse, it's time to take a long, hard look at yourself. Even 'the dog ate my football boots' is better than nothing.

Sample text message:
"Sorry mate, can't make it after all tonight."

The Crock

Has an astonishing list of ailments, which they are not afraid to pull out at strategic moments. The injuries are always mild and everyone knows that they could turn up and give it a go. Or at the very least offer to go in goals. They never do.

The Pauper

OK, we know that we are living in times of austerity, but is there ever any excuse for not being able to afford to play a game of 5-a-side? £6 is the maximum you'll pay anywhere and you've got an entire week to save for it. Have a good hunt down the back of the sofa, empty out your piggy bank, and you'll have enough to play football and get a taxi home.

Sample text message: "Sorry mate, I've tweaked my hammy / strained my ankle / picked up a groin strain."

Sample text message: "Sorry mate, things are a bit tight this month."

Have a good hunt down the back of the sofa, empty out your piggy bank, and you'll have enough to play football and get a taxi home

The Champions League Fan

This player comes into his own during the winter months, when the frost begins to bite and the prospect of playing outdoors doesn't seem so appealing. Throw in the Champions League on TV most weeks and they are likely to go into hibernation.

The Workaholic

Always seems to be caught up in some work-related crises which occurs at very late notice. Often claim they will face the sack if they don't work a late shift.

Sample text message:
"Sorry mate, PSG v Barca this week. Think I'll give football a miss."

Sample text message:
"Sorry mate, the auditors are coming in tomorrow and I need to work through the night."

The Baby-Sitter

Childcare is never an excuse for missing 5-a-side. The weekly game should be the cornerstone of your week, totally sacrosanct. Spouses should be well aware of this and work around it. If the worst comes to the worst, bring the kids along to watch.

Sample text message:
"I've got to stay in and watch my son / daughter / nephew / niece."

The One Who's Under the Thumb

He doesn't control his own leisure time, his WAG does, and his commitments to 5-a-side will always be secondary to obeying her every whim. You suspect he's fully aware of how ridiculous the situation is, but he'll never admit it. He might make a convincing fist of telling you that he really would rather spend time scrapbooking his holiday photos than playing football with his mates but everyone else just sees this as evidence of Stockholm syndrome.

Sample text message:
"Not this week, it's the Great British Bake-off final episode – me and the wife have got plans to watch it together."

The Disappearing Act

Gone from being a regular player to not turning up for football two weeks in a row. The phone number you had for them isn't working and none of the others know where he is or even why he started coming in the first place. Turns out nobody ever really knew him at all. Was he some sort of double-agent whose mission was suddenly up? Is he lying helplessly in a ditch somewhere? There's no time for investigation – he's landed you right in it, and now you've got to find a replacement player. The show must go on.

Sample text message:
"message not delivered"

Legends of
of
5-a-side
The Wizard

Meet Rob Ursell: the only one of our 5-a-side legends who ever became a full-time professional footballer, through a route that few would have expected, least of all him

Rob Ursell is a natural 5-a-side player – they call him The Wizard. Not because of his raw ability to produce magic on the court; not because he has a foot like a wand; not even because his middle name is Gandalf – actually we just made that up – but simply because his friend's dad decided to write it on a website. The name stuck, just like his deserved reputation as one of the best 5-a-side ballers out there.

He's also probably one of the only people to have represented England in three separate formats of football. Here's the legend of The Wizard.

Where did your footballing story begin?

I started off playing in a local team and when I was about seven or eight I wrote off to a load of professional clubs – pretty much every club in the top four leagues in England – to see if I could get a trial.

Most of them just ignored me but I did get a trial at Chelsea and got into their academy when I was young. That didn't last long and I got kicked out a year later because they thought I was a bit too small.

So I carried on playing Sunday league until I got another chance with a professional team, Wycombe Wanderers, when I was around 15. Unfortunately they played me as a wing-back, which really wasn't my game. I didn't have the energy or the pace for it so I didn't get offered anything there.

I played with the youth programmes of some non-league teams, but by 18 I was playing with Uxbridge Reserves and I even managed to get dropped from that, which was one of the low points of my career! So I was without a club and, whilst I hadn't consciously given up on the 11-a-side game, I wasn't thinking about playing again any time soon.

So what did you do instead?

I was just playing 5-a-side a lot at that time, with friends from school. We had decided to enter a 5-a-side league, which is where I came across this guy called Sof. At first I think we ended up arguing because he was playing against us and was absolutely destroying my mates. He told me that I was a good player but I talked too much!

Sof then asked me to come and play with him, so I did. I learned so much from him over the next couple of years. He's been the biggest influence on the way I play.

That must have been a great time, what were the things you picked up from him?

My technical ability was always better than average but it improved so much in the six months when I was playing four hours a night with Sof. We would play three or four games a night together, just finding a team to play with – there were always teams who would need players. If you practice anything enough you get good at it.

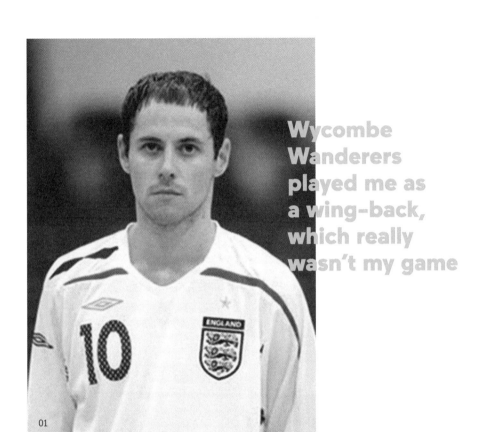

Wycombe Wanderers played me as a wing-back, which really wasn't my game

01

I signed for AFC Wimbledon where I had a couple of good years as a semi-pro

02

That time with Sof was brilliant. It's a different sort of football education than a lot of players get, but it was very valuable.

He never tried to teach me anything, never patronised me, but what he could do was amazing and I just tried to implement it and put it into my game. I couldn't do everything he could do, but I did a lot of it.

Until a couple of years ago he was probably the best player I ever played with. It was only when I ended up playing with a Brazilian futsal World Cup winner that I thought about revising that view!

But you did make it back into the 11-a-side game eventually…
Yes, I got into an 11-a-side team called Harefield Reserves through a manager that I knew and did well enough to then sign for AFC Wimbledon where I had a couple of good years as a semi-pro. I ended up leaving and never really returned to the 11-a-side game, but by that time I had started playing futsal for England.

Futsal for England, how did that come about?
AFC Wimbledon got a fax out of the blue one morning saying I was in the England futsal team. I got a call from our club secretary telling me the news that I was going to join the team for an away game against Belgium. Not even a training session, just going straight to play. I didn't even know the rules!

I had heard of futsal because my family lived in Spain where it's a big deal, but I'd never played it, never watched it in my life. I didn't even know there was an England team.

So I went to Belgium and didn't know anything tactically. I just tried to play my normal 5-a-side game, tried my skills, dribbled. If I watched myself now I'd probably ask what I was doing, but I was quite effective and managed to create a few chances.

Things went from there and I got an offer to go to Cyprus to play futsal as a full-time pro. It was a strange journey, but by signing my contract I had suddenly, at age 26, become a professional footballer for the first time.

AFC Wimbledon got a fax one morning saying I was in the England futsal team. I didn't even know the rules!

I've played futsal for England, but I've also represented the country in beach football and Minifootball [a 6-a-side format of the game] as well. Although I didn't make it to the levels in 11-a-side that I probably could have, I have a lot I can look back on, and it has been really enjoyable.

You picked up the nickname 'The Wizard' playing 11-a-side, so you can't have been bad

I was playing for the team of one of my friend's dad in Sunday league when I was about 18. He ran a website about the team, Chiswick Albion, and he just made up this nickname for me: 'The Wizard'. Nobody had ever called me that before.

After I played my first friendly for Wimbledon, all of the fans were doing internet searches to find out who I was – because I was a nobody. And that was what they found – 'The Wizard'! After that it stuck and a lot of people call me it now.

What is it about the 5-a-side game that you love?

The biggest difference is that you get so many more touches of the ball, which is obviously what skilful players like. It's an easy game to enjoy, whatever standard you play. You're much more likely to enjoy yourself playing 5-a-side in England than you are in 11-a-side. Everyone gets a touch of the ball and it's quite intense.

I've won a lot of tournaments and a lot of nice holidays with my team, MDU.

03

01 Playing for England – Ursell was recruited for the futsal team
02 Rob in action for
03 AFC Wimbledon
04 The Wizard casts his spell on another hapless defender
05 Rob in action for Omonia Nicosia in the Cypriot futsal league
06 Rob Ursell – the Wizard of Wimbledon

Individually, you need to learn how to create the space, by checking or feinting to receive the ball in all areas

So tell us about this skill that you're well known for

I used to have loads of skills, but when I came to futsal I found it's not based on dribbling as much as 5-a-side is. When I went abroad I was trying to do all these skills and my team-mates were getting really frustrated with me. So I tried to be more of a team player. It narrowed down the number of skills that I use, but I really perfected one of them in particular.

I shouldn't say it, but everyone knows I use this trick. Using the sole of my right foot I roll the ball diagonally across my body towards the defender's right foot, as if I'm going to push it past them down the line on my left side.

As their weight shifts onto their left leg so they're going to tackle with their right, my right foot goes past the ball, just about to the point of touching the ground, and with the outside of my right foot I push the ball back the other way to their left.

I usually buy myself enough space to have a shot or get past them. It creates that first bit of space that gets the defender in trouble.

My tips

Learn to move – the only reason that 5-a-side is such an individual game is that not many players learn how to move properly. If you learn to move properly it will make you a much more effective player! Individually, you need to learn how to create the space, by checking or feinting to receive the ball in all areas. The way I learned this was by trying to mark the France futsal captain. I was marking him and I never seemed to be able to find him. Afterwards I was thinking about why I spent the entire game searching for him and I realised that his movement was always away from the ball.

He made it impossible for me to see him and the ball at the same time. If you make it difficult for the defender to see you and the ball at the same time, then they panic and you can come back and find a lot of space to have the ball.

Improve your passing game – players that are very unpredictable with their dribbling are rarities. Most teams are going to work out how teams dribble and will mark the better players, sometimes putting two defenders on a player. So you have to have a good passing game to work round challenges like that.

Organise yourselves – our 5-a-side team, MDU, had a guy who for years was very good at organising us and telling us where we needed to be, particularly when we were defending. After he stopped, we didn't win anywhere near as many tournaments because we weren't as well organised defensively. Good communication makes a team very difficult to beat.

Most opponents will work out how teams dribble and mark the better players. You have to have a good passing game

AFC WIMBLEDON

Robert Ursel

06

The Wenger Principles

Do you want to become Invincible at 5-a-side? We've found the manager for you

Perhaps no manager in the history of the Premier League has celebrated the use of 5-a-side as much as Arsene Wenger. In his dynastic reign at Arsenal, generation upon generation of his teams have been raised on it.

So when he talks about 5-a-side, we should listen. And that's exactly what he did with the excellent Performance section of *Four Four Two* magazine. The result is a series of insights that should change the way you think and play – as Wenger explains, those two things are intrinsically linked.

Arsene Wenger: "5-a-side confronts the player with constant decision-making. When you receive the ball, you are faced with dozens of options. Your brain acts like a computer: it realises it has been faced with this situation before and tries to come up with the right answer – the right pass or right shot. In 5-a-side, you are faced with many of these situations, and that is why you improve so much when you play.

"I see 5-a-side as vital to coaching professionals. You may think some players who I've worked with might not be so keen on small-sided games. Where will it get them on the Saturday if it has no relevance to their usual game?

"People like Martin Keown, Tony Adams, Patrick Vieira, even Glenn Hoddle, who was such a great long passer, these guys might not have the attributes necessary to 5-a-side.

"But great players love to work and be competitive, no matter what you ask of them. Tony Adams was a fine defender, but he also liked to play. He wanted to win whenever you put him against others and by playing 5-a-side, he had an opportunity to beat others. That was very appealing to his nature."

01   Wenger decides which
team should go bibs

02   By playing 5-a-side,
Tony Adams had an
opportunity to beat
others. That appealed to
his nature

The Joy of Fives

"What attracts every player of every level is the pleasure of playing the game. By playing 5-a-side you are tapping into the roots of why they played in the first place. One day, as a kid, you played with your friends, you kicked a ball about and wow, you enjoyed it and couldn't wait to play again. By making a professional play 5-a-side you can take him back to that original joy, you can make him play with a smile on his face and that heightens his performance."

Speed of thought, speed of action

"In 5-a-side you must react quicker to things, you have to understand what is happening around you. Speed is linked with your brain. Your body must transfer your brain's decisions into actions and so speed of thought comes into play too. How quickly can you transform those messages and respond physically to them? You improve by playing. If you train for a marathon, you will be in good shape but if you come to play 5-a-side, you struggle because it's about short bursts of pace. Keep playing and that will come to you. It's all about working on your reactions."

Learn faster, get better

"How good is the quality of your touch? This can be decided from a young age, maybe as young as 12. At that age you can tell if a player is technically gifted or if they will be average for their whole life. Don't worry though, if you are average, you can still improve. By practising and playing you learn to use the ability you have in the most intelligent way. This can be learnt far easier and to greater effect by playing 5-a-side."

Finishing school

"Goalscoring can be learnt from playing and practising. Scoring is often about how much you want to score. How much does it mean to you? Take time to work on your shooting. Aim for the corners, the side netting, and your goal-scoring record will improve."

Pass first time

"In 5-a-side you don't have much time. You must be confident in making one-touch passes. Again intelligence is the key. You can find an adapted response to the situation you face. If you have that, you are on the right tracks and 5-a-side develops the speed in which you find these responses and that makes you a better passer and, in turn, a better player. The top players all know what they are going to do before they get the ball. Get a feel for having the ball at your feet while keeping your head up and your team will reap the benefits."

Personality = position

"It's important that you have the right players in the right positions. If you have doubts about what positions suit each member of your team, you might want to look at their personality. I find that quiet, efficient guys make the

best strikers. If they are cool and even a little aloof, they can be very effective up front.

Those who like to share and are more gregarious and outgoing, are made for midfield. Then you have the more aggressive ones, the type who likes to take from others, stop their progress. Make those people your defenders. If you get that right, their natural qualities develop, they become better in their positions and your team can progress and reap the benefits."

1-2-1 coaching

"Like the 11-a-side game, you do have options when it comes to picking the right formation. You can play two at the back, one in midfield and one up front, or you can have one attacker and three defenders but I

would suggest a formation that nicely marries defence with attack.

My recommended formation is 1-2-1. One defender, one attacker, with two offensive full-backs. These two players should fall back and defend when you don't have the ball but be ready to get forward and attack when necessary.

This is a formation that I feel will allow you to play the best and most effective 5-a-side. You'll be strong in defence, and dangerous in attack."

Your No.1 priority

"Try to secure a good keeper, someone not just willing to stand in the goal but who'll give you a confident last line of defence. The other option is to take it into turns but for me this is a negative tactic and doesn't allow for any cohesion. Get yourself a goalkeeper.

In front of your goalie, you need a good defender. This position is very important. Not only should this player be willing to block, tackle and spoil, he or she must also be comfortable starting attacks and therefore should be a decent passer.

I like to think of the defender as a quarterback type of player. If you get it right, you can be the player who dictates the team's performance."

Play on the break...

"If you watch 5-a-side, most goals will come from a quick burst upfield. One or two passes and then shoot. It is the teams that have too much of the ball and are playing too many passes amongst themselves that have the least success. Be quick, be ruthless and you'll be successful.

By sitting back and defending you are tempting your opposition to lose their shape, frustrating them, before winning the ball and scoring on the break. But to do it well, the two full-back-midfield players are vital. They must support the defender and nullify the other team, but in a flash, break out and get among the goals."

... and play for the team

"Attacking egos must be left in the dressing room. Your striker needs to have a lot to his or her game. They must be eager to get in behind and to score goals, of course, but in 5-a-side they must also be very unselfish. They must be able to play with their back to goal, bring in the attacking full-backs with little wall passes.

You are always susceptible to a goal on the break and should guard against it. So attack as a team but always leave a player safely at the back. It doesn't have to be the defender: don't be rigid, but be safe."

Enjoy the game

"The last bit of advice I can give is to go out and enjoy yourself. There's nothing better than playing the game with your mates, giving it your all, hopefully winning and then going for a drink afterwards.

That doesn't have to be alcoholic drink, by the way. But if you must, go on – you deserve it."

*This interview was first published by Four Four Two Performance. You can get many more great tips on improving your game and your fitness by following them on Facebook and Twitter and keeping up to date with their content online and in the magazine

Shooting

Everything you know is wrong

When it comes to shooting in 5-a-side, remember the old Pirelli Tyres tagline: Power is nothing without control.

Why? Well, think about the move from 11-a-side to 5-a-side. Your target – the goal – just shrank. But the obstacle – the goalkeeper – remains the same size.

Kurtice Herbert, perhaps the most prolific player in elite 5-a-side in the UK, puts it like this:

> "I rarely lace it when I'm shooting, instead I prefer to side-foot the ball into the corner. With your laces you'll hit a spot say four times out of 10, but with your side foot, it's more like seven."

You have to be able to hit the corners. Practicing that one technique will have a dramatic impact on your goalscoring stats. Learn to do it from an angle, on the move, with both feet and under pressure.

Finally, keep your shots low. In 11-a-side, the top corner of the goal is a tough place for keepers to get to, and there can be value in aiming high and hitting it hard. In fives, the risk-reward ratio of a high shot makes it a terrible option. Every shot that clears the bar is a crime.

Aim low and aim true.

TO SCALE:

11-A-SIDE GOAL SIZE
(24FT X 8FT)

5-A-SIDE GOAL SIZE
(16FT X 4FT)

5-a-side

Tales from the pitch

The Business Cup

By Graham Broadley

We once held a 'Business Cup' for a mix of companies – retailers, accountants etc – from the local area. There was a guy from a car firm who entered a team and made it through to the final, with him playing in goal. They were 3-0 up, everything was looking good and this guy started to get a bit cocky.

Then they conceded a strange goal, where the ball hit the post and then went in off his backside. 3-1. The opposition pulled two more goals back and suddenly it was 3-3. Game on.

Then events took an astonishing turn. The goalie went to throw the ball out to one of his team-mates, then changed his mind at the last second; in doing so, he somehow spun round and threw the ball into his own goal.

Immediately, he turned to the referee: "That doesn't count, that can't happen." The referee correctly said: "Yes it can, it's full-time and you've lost 4-3."

The guy went mental and squared up but the referee just couldn't stop laughing and walked back inside the clubhouse. The goalie chased him all the way into the clubhouse, but to no avail.

Then, he started literally crying to one of the centre managers until his less-than-sympathetic team-mates led him away. "This would have been the best cup I've ever won in my life. I could've gone home and showed my wife and kids." He was a 50-year-old man.

The Remarkables

How do you make the most of your 5-a-side team using technology and social media? We think this lot have got it sussed

01

Meet The Remarkables.

The story of this women's team from South Africa is nothing short of inspirational. It combines the best use of social media and technology we have seen in 5-a-side, some breath-taking locations, cutting-edge training and performance analysis, and a group of footballers who have fun, win, and tell their story brilliantly online.

And they achieved all of this from a standing start.

Their coach, Taz Raza, moved to South Africa from the UK in 1999 and works for Prozone in Cape Town, giving The Remarkables a handy edge in the tech stakes. We caught up with Taz for the low down on a unique 5-a-side story.

Tell us how the team came together and your role in it...

After the 2010 World Cup a group of girls from the Architecture Masters Class at UCT (University of Cape Town) decided they wanted to learn how to play football.

02

As they all went to traditional schools where football was not played by girls they had to ask one of the boys in their class, Mark, to show them how.

The team grew very quickly to around 16 girls and they asked a local coaching company called Mind, Body and Goal to step in and structure sessions in a way that gradually improved the girls' technical abilities and tactical awareness.

We train once a week on a Sunday at a local 5-a-side pitch next to Cape Town's 2010 World Cup stadium

I started coaching the ladies through Mind, Body and Goal in 2012, soon after completing my introductory coaching badge through SAFA and the Introduction to Futsal Coaching through FutsalSA.

My aim was to take my knowledge of football and integrate it with something that I felt was lacking in the South African game: video feedback. I wanted to see how adding this element would improve the ladies' game and at what rate. I experimented with various types of feedback and we're now at a stage where information is stored, packaged and fed back to the ladies in a quick, informative way. This has led to the ladies going from simply wanting to learn how to play football to winning competitions in the space of just three years.

How seriously do you take it? It looks like you train regularly and have enjoyed some success. Tell us about that...
The Remarkables are a combination of young professionals and students with ages ranging from 16-32.

We train once a week on a Sunday at a local 5-a-side pitch next to Cape Town's 2010 World Cup Stadium. We also arrange weekly friendly matches against men's teams which provides an added challenge. The increase in tempo and intensity of these sessions help the team cope with playing under pressure and helps them prepare them for league matches against tougher opposition.

Although the social games are always enjoyable, we prefer the competitive element of playing in a league.

It looks like you have put the players through some Prozone analysis...
Prozone recently released software known as GameLens which I was fortunate to test in the build up to its release. The tool is great in that it allows me as the coach to review video footage of games, create my own tagging

template to tag specific events that I feel the ladies need to be aware of and also gives me the ability to cut and export clips easily. This can be fed back to the team in the lead up to their next game in the form of two or three simple clips. We post some of this information on our Twitter feed as well.

Having the ladies re-watch their footage gives them an added advantage in that they make more immediate adjustments to their game and can monitor their improvements.

Next season, I'll be looking to use the software to tag, or code, key match stats after each game such as shots, assists and interceptions. We will also look to include things like areas of the pitch where possession is lost or won. Pitch maps of actions are another great way to visualise information and can reinforce a point. This data can give us trends and we can then put together more detailed player profile cards.

This can all take some time!

Talk us through the social media – you have brilliant Twitter and Instagram accounts, you have some video on there too...
As we film all our games for feedback purposes, I thought it would be a great opportunity to use this footage to increase the appeal of women's football in Cape Town through our social media accounts.

In addition to this, our accounts can be used as a platform to advertise our future tournaments, and we are hoping to secure a local sponsor to help us with the financial side of the club.

Internationally, we can also keep up to date with what's happening around the world in women's football and find some great resources to help further our game.

As our accounts grow, we will always look to evolve the content and share what we can with others on social media platforms.

Are there many women playing football and 5-a-side in South Africa?
South Africa has an 11-a-side league knows as the Sasol League which is SAFA accredited. It was formed in 2009, there are currently around 144 teams.

Our national women's team, Banyana Banyana, are yet to compete in a World Cup, but have recently qualified for the All Africa Games which will be held in Congo in September. They have also just advanced to the third round of qualifiers for the Rio Olympics. Qualification into big tournaments will increase the exposure of the women's team throughout the country.

We hope that the interest in 5-a-side grows as it's a great format for newcomers and perhaps less intimidating than playing 11-a-side straight away.

There are currently two 5-a-side leagues in Cape Town that allocate one day of the week to women's football. Many of the players play 11-a-side and it's a great opportunity to keep playing during the off-season. There's some seriously talented players out there.

There is also a great love for football in the less fortunate areas of Cape Town and a huge demand for well-run facilities and programmes. Once girls reach a certain age, usually their early teens, there is a massive decline in their attendance due to socio-economic reasons.

With the correct support, we can positively influence these young women's lives by not only nurturing great footballing talent, but also providing valuable life skills and access to health education, women's rights and further educational and mentoring programmes.

We've seen the pitch in the shadow of Table Mountain. Tell us about some of the other spectacular locations...
We're surrounded by natural beauty and fortunate enough to have the incredible backdrop of the stadium with Table Mountain on one side and the ocean on the other. You can understand why Cape Town is affectionately known as 'The Mother City'.

There are a handful of 5-a-side sites in Cape Town and each has a very unique feel and incredible backdrops. I would recommend anyone who loves the game to visit any of these sites when in Cape Town to experience some local flavour.

You can find The Remarkables...
On Twitter: @RemarkablesFC
On Instagram: @remarkablesfc

01   The Remarkables

02   The Remarkables being put through their paces

03   Coach Taz Raza delivers a team talk

03

Know Your Role

Goalkeeper: A good goalkeeper will hide a multitude of defensive sins and keep you in games you would otherwise lose. A bad goalkeeper, on the other hand, will undermine everything good that the rest of the team tries to do and sap the confidence and motivation from the team. In 45 minutes of 5-a-side football, a goalkeeper will face around five times the number of on-target shots he or she would see in 90 minutes of 11-a-side.

Last man: This player is going to be responsible and disciplined. They'll show strong players on to their weak side. They will hold up counter-attacks, even 2-on-1s, allowing their team-mates to get back into position. It's also vital that they move up now and again, keeping the opposition pivot honest and providing an unexpected, late-arriving goal threat.

Pivot: The primary source of goals, the pivot will know how to make the most out of the slightest opportunity. They've also got to be able to play with their back to goal, providing a strong target for a pass to their feet, and knowing when to play in their supporting players.

The other guys: The wider players in this formation have the hardest shift ahead of them. They have to transition quickly between defence and attack. A strong player in one of these positions isn't going to have as much of an impact on the game as they would in one of the central positions, but if one of these two doesn't have the fitness or the attitude to work for the team, everybody else will suffer.

Gascoigne V Charlton

5-a-side
Dream Team

Our Verdict – Charlton win

Gazza's lack of defensive nous and blind loyalty to the Geordie nation leaves his team vulnerable to the wizardry of Best and Matthews

○
David Seaman

○
Chris Waddle

○
Paul Gascoigne

○
Kenny Wharton

○
Peter Beardsley

○
Duncan Edwards

○
George Best

○
Stanley Matthews

○
Ray Wilson

○
Gordon Banks

Block Party

How to get better at goalkeeping

It has been said that a 5-a-side goalkeeper accounts for as much as 60% of the success of the entire team. Debate the number all you want, but the majority of players would agree: it's the most important position on the pitch

The goalkeeper is the last line of defence, the guardian of the gate through which the ball must not pass. Do that job well and you're a hero, but if you get it wrong it's a different story. Your team-mates' criticism is only tempered by the fact that none of them want to go in goal instead.

Goalkeeping duties in 5-a-side are all too often assigned to a reluctant outfield player, and it's one of the main reasons why teams lose games. If you haven't got a specialist keeper who wants to play in goal, it's going to undermine a lot of the good work that the rest of the team does.

Whether you're playing there because you love it, or whether you're the reluctant stand-in, knowing the keys of good 5-a-side goalkeeping can dramatically improve your performance and transform you from a blundering butterfingers into the cat-like king of the court.

Meet the Experts
Who better to guide you through the finer points of goalkeeping than two 5-a-side masters – you'll see their tips below.

Ashoor   The Cat

Roger Paul Noveal/The Cat – The man who they know on the 5-a-side circuit quite simply as 'The Cat'. With nearly 20 years' experience playing in goal for some of the best 5-a-side teams, and winning multiple national titles, he's seen it all.

Ashoor – Goalkeeper for the most successful 5-a-side team of 2014, West 13. These guys won almost every major tournament that could be won, and it was thanks in no small part to having a quality goalkeeper between the sticks.

So, let's get on to looking at the key ingredients of top 5-a-side goalkeeping:

1. Focus

5-a-side isn't like the 11-a-side game. The biggest difference for a goalkeeper – and also what makes so many of them love the smaller format – is the huge increase in workload. Players can, and very often do, shoot from absolutely anywhere.

In the Premier League 2014/15 season, teams took an average of around 13 shots per 90-minute game. Only four of them were on target, leaving the goalkeeper with lots of quiet periods. In 5-a-side barely a minute goes by where you aren't called into action.

5-a-side goalkeeping should be every bit as exhausting as being an outfield player because you need to be alert all the time; constantly re-positioning yourself as the play unfolds. Get on your toes and be ready at any moment.

The Cat

The Cat Says: Anyone can lose the ball, at any time. If they do, you have to be ready to make a big save when your opponents break. When your team attacks, be prepared for that counter. Hope for the best but prepare for the worst.

Ashoor

Ashoor Says: 11-a-side goalkeepers should get involved with more 5-a-side because it really improves your reactions, movement and awareness. In 11-a-side you're not getting tested two or three times every minute.

2. Bravery

The 5-a-side goalkeeper has to be ready to put his body on the line. A lot of the time we're not talking about glamorous, full-stretch, fingertip saves, as seen on TV. Most of the shots coming a 5-a-side goalkeeper's way are struck from close range, and are saved by instinctive reactions. Shots are fired at your body, your legs, your head, and eventually any keeper worth his salt will end up taking a couple in the crown jewels, too.

Getting enough padding and wearing finger-protection gloves can help players feel more comfortable, but at the end of the day it's more about having the minerals for the job. You're going to need balls the size of coconuts. Coconuts made of steel.

If you're fearful of doing whatever it takes to keep the ball out of your net, you might as well give up now.

The Cat

The Cat Says: Players will strike the ball so hard from point blank range and if you're not brave, you'll pull out and they'll score. From that point, they'll smell your fear, and then they've got you. I don't care what injury I get as long as I don't let them score. I've saved a fair few penalties with my face!

3. Positioning

5-a-side goals might not be tall but they can still be very wide, up to 16ft. So even with an enormous reach you're still going to be beaten by shots into the corner if you stay on your line:

Fortunately, the 5-a-side goalkeeper usually has a D-shaped area in which he operates, and this should be used to its full extent. If there's an opponent bearing down on goal, you want to be right out on the edge of the area shutting down the angle.

The Cat

The Cat Says: 5-a-side goals are smaller than 11-a-side goals, but if your positioning isn't good, you'll be picking the ball out of the net all too often. My golden rule is that you should never get

beaten on your near post. When a player goes down either wing you might need to take one or two steps off your line so that you don't get caught on the near post or across your goal – players are often taught to shoot across the goal.

Ashoor

Ashoor Says: you have to know when to come out and how to make the angle to give yourself a chance to stop them scoring. These shots are coming at you at such a fast pace and sometimes it might just hit your body and that's still a save, but it only comes about because of your positioning.

4. Technique

When it comes to 5-a-side goalkeeping there are a few specialist skills that you need to learn:

Stay low so that you're ready to deal with any shots that come your way: the 5-a-side keeper has the luxury not to need to worry about shots above waist-height. If you're beaten it will be low-down, and if your stance is bolt-upright it's going to take you longer to get down to any shots.

Understand the difference between blocking and saving: 'Saving' is where you're dealing with shots coming from distance – where you get at least a split second to think about how you might deal with it, often diving to get a hand on it. 'Blocking' is the more common technique for 5-a-side and that's where you simply throw yourself in front of a shot – nearly always from close-range – trying to give them as little of the goal as possible to aim for. Blocking can be done by going to ground, or by taking up more of a kneeling position (the advantage being that it's easier to react to the shot-fake in the latter position). Pick a blocking technique that works for you and develop it – it's going to be a vital part of your goalkeeping toolkit.

Make maximum use of your feet: There isn't time to think about most of the shots that come your way, and in a lot of cases you won't even have time to dive. It's often a lot quicker to stretch a leg out to the side than it is to dive down to make the save with your hand. If you can turn your feet outwards as you make contact then this should allow you to get a solid block on the ball, repelling it well away from the goal.

Ashoor

Ashoor Says: Some of the shots are coming from less than five yards away and they're being blasted with as much power as they can possibly generate so it's impossible to catch them. It's a very low percentage of shots that you'll actually catch during a game. It's more important to just get something on it and stop the ball going in the net. If you catch it, that's a bonus.

> 'Blocking' is the more common technique for 5-a-side and that's where you simply throw yourself in front of a shot – trying to give them as little of the goal as possible to aim for

3 METHODS OF BLOCKING

5. Agility

It goes without saying that the more agile you are, the quicker you can respond to shots, even dodgy deflections, that come your way.

The Cat

The Cat Says: Here's a great drill to improve your agility as a 5-a-side keeper. Get a player to hit the ball low to your left so that by diving you'll get a hand to it – no need to catch it, just get a hand to turn it round the post. Then repeat, and each time get slightly faster so that eventually you're diving and the ball flies past your hand because you aren't fast enough to get down to the ground. Do 10 of these on your left and then the same on the right side.

6. Communication & Organisation

If a goalkeeper can communicate effectively with his teammates – in a clear and helpful way – he can snuff out shots before they've even been taken. This involves ensuring that your players don't switch off, and that they pick up the opposition players. Crucially, you don't want your team-mates to let the other team have any shooting opportunities that come from the middle of the pitch – instead, encourage them to show their opponents wide, where you have a much better chance of narrowing the angle and making the save.

Coach one or two trusty defenders to respond to your instructions. When the ball gets anywhere near your area, they almost become keepers themselves, throwing their body in the way to make the block.

Ashoor

Ashoor Says: There are times when you'll concede a goal and your player will look round as if to say 'come on, you could've saved that', but they don't think that a moment or two before that they could've stopped it happening. Even when the opposition's keeper has got the ball, I'm trying to think how I can help my team-mates to stop them from getting a shot on me. That's especially important in a tense match where players are so focused on their own game that they switch off.

The Cat

The Cat Says: As a keeper you see everything and, if you can, tell your team-mates what's going on. Just a little call like 'man on' or 'time' will really help them. The better you can help them play, the easier your job is.

7. Distribution

For every wonder-save that gets made on the 5-a-side court, there's another goal that's given away from poor distribution. You know the situation: the keeper is looking around thinking 'who do I throw it out to?' but none of his team-mates seem to be moving. Eventually out of impatience he chucks it at one of his players who loses it and the opposition end up scoring a cheap goal.

Getting distribution right is about three things: players moving for you, having the patience to wait for this to happen (or at least giving them this instruction), and then giving them a quality roll-out.

Ashoor

Ashoor Says: When I've got the ball, sometimes everyone just runs towards me, but I'm not giving it to anyone whilst they're all on top of me. It only takes a second to lose it and I might concede a goal. Talking to the players and telling them you want one left, one right, one up top and one in the middle helps. I see so many keepers with the ball just looking round, not even talking, then they just roll it out into trouble and the next thing a goal goes in. That's so disheartening.

The Cat

The Cat Says: If you can distribute the ball correctly, your player can strike that ball before he's even controlled it. Make sure that the player receiving it gets it exactly the way he wants it, give it to his stronger foot and make sure that it rolls nice and flat along the floor. Think about the action for flat-green bowling: it's perfect. You release the ball nice and low to the floor, so that from the moment it leaves your hand it's already rolling nice and flat. A lot of the keepers are just chucking it at their players giving them a bouncing ball. Pass it to them in a smooth, flowing way so they don't have to spend time controlling it.

> Make sure that the player receiving it gets it exactly the way he wants it, give it to his stronger foot and make sure that it rolls nice and flat along the floor

How to score at penalties

Ben Lyttleton wrote the book on penalties – scoring them, saving them, the psychology and the science. He gives us his expert advice

The penalty is football in its basic form: the ball, the goal, a striker and a goalkeeper. You often hear players talk about how the goal shrinks when they are taking a high-pressure penalty, but when it comes to the 5-a-side format, that is more true still. And the goal is smaller to begin with.

However, there are still plenty of tactics to get a competitive advantage over your rivals when it comes to 5-a-side spot-kicks. Here are a few that could help your team:

Take your time:
Waiting one extra second after the referee blows his whistle to denote the penalty can be taken could make all the difference. Based on analysis of reaction times from the referee blowing his whistle to players beginning their run-up, England national team players wait an average 0.28 seconds. This is quicker than any other nation, and a sure sign of stress. It's not far off Usain Bolt, whose average reaction time is 0.18 seconds.

Personality is no guide to success:
You might think that a player with a confident personality would do better from the spot, but that's not right. An academic study carried out in Germany, called 'The Penalty King of Leipzig', discovered that the greatest marker for success was nothing to do with self-confidence or even innate football ability, but all about competition anxiety, which is simply how well you perform under pressure. Introverts with low anxiety perform far better than extroverts with high anxiety.

Aiming high gives you more chance to miss:

'The arc of uncertainty' is a semi-circle that starts about half a foot inside each post and circles its way around the goal: kick the ball anywhere outside the arc (but inside the posts) and your penalty will be impossible to save. For 11-a-side goals, the greatest space outside the arc is in the top corners: for 5-a-side goals, there is far less margin for error. The top corner is a small one and easily missed. It's a question of pure maths: you can hit the ball too high, but you can never hit it too low. So aiming low and into a corner is the best option for 5-a-side.

Don't over-think it:

A neurological professor divided a roomful of golfers in two, and had them all holing putts from the same distance. They then had a five-minute break, during which half the golfers wrote down every aspect of their putts, and the other half looked at pictures of beaches and cars. They all then putted again, and the golfers who had focused on the golf in the break all hit far worse putts second time around. What does this have to do with penalties? It shows that over-thinking a task can lead to a negative result – so players need to have a strategy of what to think about before striking the ball.

To wait or not wait?
The two distinct strategies for penalty-takers are as follows:

Goalkeeper-Dependent involves a slow run-up, waiting for the goalkeeper to make the first move, and then rolling the ball in the other direction. Stars of this strategy include Eden Hazard, Yaya Toure, Matt Le Tissier and Gaizka Mendieta. The other method is **Goalkeeper-Independent**, which is basically picking a spot and smashing the ball there (often off a faster run-up). This works for Alan Shearer, Rickie Lambert and Arturo Vidal. Which is better? Over time, Goalkeeper-Dependent is more successful, but be warned that the technique is harder, and needs to be practised rigorously.

Ben Lyttleton is the author of the definitive book on penalty kicks in all modes of football, *Twelve Yards: The Art & Psychology of the Perfect Penalty*

You've read the book – now don't lose your touch.

Get great 5-a-side content like this all year round at 5-a-side.com.

Go there now for fresh tips on tactics, fitness and nutrition as well as more of the humour that makes fives more than a game.

And join the mailing list to be part of the biggest and fastest-growing 5-a-side community on the internet.

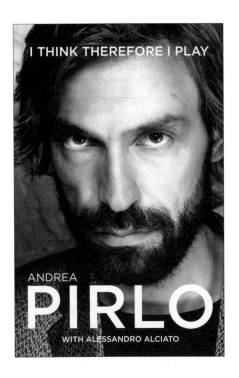

I THINK THEREFORE I PLAY

ANDREA
PIRLO

WITH ALESSANDRO ALCIATO

Football Manager Stole My Life reveals the cult behind a computer game that since its debut in 1992, has sold 20m copies and become a part of football culture.

Acknowledgments

Thanks to everybody who made this book possible. From ex-pros to casual players; from sports scientists to referees, thank you to everybody who gave their time so generously just to chat about 10 people kicking a ball around. Pope John Paul II is attributed to have said that "of all the unimportant things, football is the most important" and this book has proved he got it spot on (although I'm not sure he would've picked the title we went with – no offence intended!)

5-a-side really is the people's game and people just love to talk about it. Special thanks to the legends for giving away all their trade secrets and particularly to Roger Paul Noveal, who made it possible to track down even the slipperiest of slippery interviewees with his extensive contacts.

Shout out to all the Tuesday-night football gang (Clontarf – 30-odd years and counting), who helped out with the cover photoshoot on a chilly Glasgow night. You're all 5-a-side legends.

Thanks also to Martin and Neil at BackPage for all their excellent edits, articles, and for being passionate enough to make this book a reality.

Lastly, thanks to the many characters of the 5-a-side world – it takes all comers and it wouldn't be the same without you all. Whatever your standard, whatever your motivation, seeing millions of you turn out on a freezing Thursday night in November is inspiration for us all.